M000103632

Hope in Times of Darkness

A Salvadoran American Experience

Randy Jurado Ertll

Hamilton Books
A member of
The Rowman & Littlefield Publishing Group
Lanham • Boulder • New York • Toronto • Plymouth, UK

Copyright © 2009 by
Hamilton Books
4501 Forbes Boulevard
Suite 200
Lanham, Maryland 20706
Hamilton Books Acquisitions Department (301) 459-3366

Estover Road
Plymouth PL6 7PY
United Kingdom

Library of Congress Control Number: 2009930998
ISBN: 978-0-7618-4666-6 (paperback : alk. paper)
eISBN: 978-0-7618-4667-3

To my mother,
two sisters,
Karen,
my sweet daughter Mirian,
and Mama Gume.

Contents

Foreword by
Ramon C. Cortines

The journey of Randy Jurado Ertll has not been easy by any means. He grew up in El Salvador and South Central Los Angeles. He lived in dangerous and violent environments. He overcame many challenges through focusing on obtaining a quality education through the Los Angeles Unified School District and through the A Better Chance scholarship program. He sacrificed by going away to Rochester, Minnesota and leaving his mother and two younger sisters behind. But he needed to get away, to escape the allure of gangs.

Jurado Ertll sets an example that minority youth who grow up in the inner-city can in fact become successful and should return to their own communities to make a significant and positive impact in improving the lives of others. He has done an excellent job being executive director of El Centro de Accion Social where he helps countless students and senior citizens through social service programs. He is committed to social justice.

Jurado Ertll witnessed much violence and injustices. Instead of giving up or being intimidated, he has stood up and fought for the rights of others. It is an exhausting and demanding journey, but we need community leaders like him to continue making social change.

His story transcends the Salvadoran American experience. It is a real life story of perseverance and courage. As a Mexican American myself, I understand his struggles and dreams. Thousands of young students will relate to his story, will gain insight, and knowledge of opportunities that do exist to help our students. Our students need to be aware of the various programs that are available to help them succeed. We cannot afford to allow "our children" to drop out or join gangs.

They must seek the path of knowledge. As Superintendent of the Los Angeles Unified School District I applaud Randy's efforts to inform our community through this insightful and powerful book. We have to teach our children that there is "Hope in Times of Darkness."

Ramon (Ray) Cortines
Superintendent of the Los Angeles Unified School District (LAUSD).

Acknowledgments

I would like to especially thank the following individuals who have been friends and supportive through the journey of this book—Matt Rothschild, Luke Williams, Betsy Lordan, Judy Martinez, Roger Atwood, Earl Ofari Hutchinson, Nora Hamilton, Tony Garcia, Lisa Ramos, Blanca and Rene Polio, Rolando and Reina Castillo, Mauricio Cienfuegos, Warren Montag, Patrick O'Brien, Dolores Huerta, Margaret Crahan, Raheema Sameem, Louis DeSipio, Barbara Villasenor, Marvin Andrade, Hilda Solis, Monica Lozano, Henrik Rehbinder, Roger Lindo, Ramon Cortines, Scott Forrey, Rampa Hormel, Trent and Becky Fluegel, and the staff of El Centro de Accion Social. My family members who live in California, Washington D.C., Virginia, Florida, and El Salvador. Thank you to all of my other friends who have helped me along the way and who believe in the full potential of children, regardless of their background. Finally, I would like to especially thank Brooke Bascietto for accepting my initial query and my manuscript. Writing is lonely and has to be done with passion – it is not for the faint of heart. Thank you to those individuals who read my manuscript and provided feedback. May God bless all of my friends and family, thank you for believing in me.

Introduction

Growing Up in
South Central Los Angeles

KIDS SHOULDN'T HAVE TO FLEE L.A. TO HAVE HOPE
By Randy Jurado Ertll. Published in the Los Angeles Times.

The inner city was my neighborhood. In the 1980s, when I was attending junior high school in South Central Los Angeles, gang violence was common and respect for teachers was absent. Being a victim of senseless street conflict was something I worked to avoid.

I immersed myself in books, in reading and writing. My first triumph was in eighth grade. I won a school essay contest and $100 was the prize. My subject was George Washington Carver. My mother was quite proud of my writing achievement.

And it was an achievement. I was born in Los Angeles. When I was 8 months old, U.S. immigration agents arrested my mother and deported her back to El Salvador. She had no choice but to take me with her. We didn't return until I was 5. At school I was considered an immigrant. It wasn't until the fourth grade that I learned to read and write in English.

In junior high school, the so-called smart students were invited to attend a workshop about a national program called A Better Chance, or ABC. It provided scholarships for students to attend excellent schools far from the inner city. It was during a time when I felt pressure to join a gang. I saw ABC as my big opportunity to escape, and I applied to Deerfield Academy in Massachusetts, as far away as I could go.

ABC sent me a typed letter saying I wasn't selected. I wrote back, in long hand, asking why. It had created and then crushed my hope, I wrote. Save me, I pleaded. ABC officials phoned me. The conversation is still vivid in my memory. They said I was accepted into the program after all and could attend an academy in Rochester, Minn.

The airplane ticket arrived and I was gone. I left my mother and two sisters behind. That was heartbreaking. As the family's only boy, I saw myself as its protector, though the reality was I couldn't even protect myself.

Except for one Mexican American boy from East Los Angeles, my housemates in Minnesota were nearly all African American. We went through difficult times learning to accept one another. In South Central L.A., blacks and Latinos competed for scarce economic and political resources, but at John Marshall High School in Rochester we learned to care for and respect each other. I grew close to my house directors, who were white. Ethnicity didn't matter.

As a senior in 1991, I read a pamphlet that said Occidental College, in the Eagle Rock area of Los Angeles, placed an emphasis on learning about multicultural issues. I applied and was accepted. Majoring in politics with a minor in Spanish, I graduated from Occidental with distinction in 1995.

Now I think back to that critical stage in my life when the ABC program removed me from my environment to prepare me to attend college, to succeed. It assured me I had the capacity to do it. No one could make me feel inferior. In a nation built by immigrants, I learned to find pride in my immigrant family.

A Better Chance turned my dreams into reality. I became a role model in my family and my community. I worked in the environmental movement, in immigrant rights advocacy and in Washington as a communications director and legislative assistant to Rep. Hilda L. Solis (D-El Monte). Each one helped shape who I am today.

Now I live in Pasadena, some areas of which are not that different from South Central Los Angeles. Many of the students I see daily remind me of myself when I was going through similar struggles. The job of public school districts is to offer them a better chance, a quality education and hope, without their having to travel halfway across the country.

Randy Jurado Ertll
Graduate of A Better Chance (ABC)
scholarship program and alumnus
of Occidental College

Chapter One

The Story of a
Salvadoran American

Escaping a Civil War and landing in another one: it's not what a five-year-old child expects.

Yet again nothing in life is easy, especially while being deported to El Salvador as an eight month old baby with my mother. Immigration agents arrested my mother while she worked at a sweatshop in downtown Los Angeles. They could care less that my mother had an eight month old baby. Immigration laws were and still are inhumane.

I have been told that when we landed in El Salvador, my grandparents were waiting for us and I reached out to hug my grandfather. As an adult, I cannot remember my grandfather's face, since I was only four years old when he passed away. But he taught me about love, humility, and hard work. He was the Salvadoran version of Cesar Chavez. He believed in fairness and justice for the working-class. I still remember his funeral and how I threw a handful of dirt into his grave, as a way of saying good bye.

My grandfather and grandmother had 11 other children besides my mother. My grandpa was a carpenter and a farmer. My grandpa worked the land all of his life and raised his sons and daughters under extreme hardships. He was a man of honesty and integrity. My grandma represents the struggle of the Salvadoran woman—always working and providing for their children. However, the cruel Civil War did take away a son from my grandma. My uncle was reported to have been tortured and murdered. His body was never found. My grandma still waits for his return. She says "donde esta mi hijito?" (where is my son) to this day.

Hundreds of years before, the Spanish colonizers had established a system of exploitation through the ownership of massive plots of land where the indigenous and mestizos of the peasant class labored under grueling conditions, just to survive. But the indigenous people of El Salvador (Los Pipiles) are tough. They resisted Spanish conquest for years while other countries were already being converted to Catholicism and other traditions imposed by the Spanish. Unfortunately, the Spanish soldiers were better armed and brought many diseases, and they finally conquered Los Pipiles. The Spanish colonizers became experts at pitting different tribes to fight against each other. Even though the Pipiles were conquered, the resilient spirit remained within the Salvadoran people.

After gaining its independence from Spain, what is now considered Central America was then a federation of states, which later gained independence becoming sovereign states. Historically, El Salvador is noted as being a leader to first seek independence and sovereignty. Unfortunately, the countries within the Central American Federation adopted the political and economic examples set by Spain, where a very few wealthy individuals, the oligarchs, owned most of the land, creating a class disparity, which continued to be replicated throughout the 20th Century and to present day El Salvador. Let us revisit some of the recent history of this small resilient country.

The 1970s were a decade of economic desperation and the U.S. energy crisis forced Americans to stop funding certain development programs that benefited the most disadvantaged citizens of El Salvador. President Kennedy's "Alliance for Progress," which consisted of a program to help the very poor with food and other basic resources, came to an abrupt end in Latin America. The policy behind the "Alliance for Progress" was to provide funding to Latin American countries to counter Communist influence. The governments from these Latin American countries had to agree to implement policies/reforms imposed by the United States. Some of these countries refused to implement certain reforms. Also, funding for the Alliance for Progress was diverted since the U.S. had to fund the Vietnam War. The Alliance for Progress program ended in 1973.

In the 70s, thousands of young students, professors, intellectuals, and campesinos became increasingly frustrated with the Salvadoran government. Several future guerrilla comandantes of the FMLN (Farabundo Marti para la Liberacion Nacional) were students attending the Universidad Nacional de El Salvador or La UCA (the Jesuit-influenced Central American University). There they became politically involved in efforts to improve the lives of the most disadvantaged.

While many believed that these young men and women were becoming influenced by socialist and communist theories from Russia, China, Vietnam, and Cuba, others believed that these young intellectuals were simply seeking a more equitable society. Many political activists believed that social justice could only be achieved through armed struggle. Many of them lost their lives in aims to achieve political change through their ideologies.

Fighting this war meant 12-years of death and destruction leaving unforgettable moments for every Salvadoran that one way or the other lived the pain of losing someone they loved. Many guerrillas throughout Latin America romanticized and idealized Fidel Castro and Che Guevara's political theories. The death of "El Che" was later noted to have been a betrayal by being left alone to fight a guerrilla war in Bolivia with only a handful of followers. Che believed in helping the underdog and he gave his life fighting for revolution. His death was cruel and lonely.

Also, some of the Salvadoran guerrillas did not take into account that a U.S. Republican President, Ronald Reagan, was to determine the course of U.S. foreign policy in the 1980s. He had zero tolerance for communist agitators and was willing to do anything to stop the so-called Communist threat. Reagan became known as a no non-sense type of leader who was willing to use any type of force to stop Communism.

I was a child during the 1970s and my world was a magical place filled with trees, birds, mountains, and a beautiful stream that ran near our house in the countryside of Usulutan, El Salvador. Once in a while my mother would take me to San Salvador while she worked at the Almacenes SIMAN. My mother taught me the ethic of hard work, to be an honest person, and to always believe in myself. In El Salvador, she worked with the Siman's family, who were immigrants from Palestine and who migrated to El Salvador as business people.

I still remember the smell of fried beans, nuegados from El Mercado Central and the smell of diesel from the buses. I remember the fusion of smells from the marketplace and the sales ladies shouting the various bargains. Some of those same ladies still work at the Mercado. Of course, they have aged tremendously. You can see the toll that the sun has taken on their skin and how the Civil War took away their optimism.

El Salvador continues to be a country that's always buzzing with activity. Its people have a reputation for being hard workers, so Japan, Taiwan and other foreign countries have invested heavily to make the most of its cheap and efficient labor. Of course, one could argue that while multinational corporations and foreign investors benefit greatly, the poor are exploited.

The mentality of colonization and economic exploitation has not changed much since the arrival of the Spaniards. Thousands of Salvadorans are now exploited in the maquilas where they are forced to work extremely long hours with little pay and no benefits. That is what global capitalism has created. Most of the workers get paid less than $5 a day with no benefits such as health insurance or vacation time. Many of the maquila's workers allege a diverse number of violations. The exploitation of the Salvadoran people has historical roots.

El Salvador can indeed distinguish itself as a country that initially managed to resist-Spanish colonization. But the bloodshed did not end there. In 1932, more than 30,000 indigenous people were murdered during "La Matanza." General Maximiliano Martinez decided to stop all Communist influence and activities and wanted to set an example by capturing a campesino leader, Farabundo Marti. Essentially, he used the "Communist" threat as an excuse to eradicate most indigenous people from El Salvador, and to justify taking land from the indigenous people.

The violence brought by Spanish conquistadores like Pedro de Alvarado in the 1500s was matched by the Salvadoran military in the 1930s. Pedro de Alvarado was a cruel and heartless Conquistador. He enjoyed torturing and murdering the indigenous population. The cruel and violent history of El Salvador set the stage for what was to come in the 1980s.

Fortunately for me, by then my mother had already decided to bring me back to the United States. We were still living in El Salvador when we attended a protest on February 28, 1977 at the Plaza de Libertad. Hundreds of innocent civilians were gunned down and murdered by the military that day. Water hoses were used to clean up the blood, and the bodies were taken away. The next day, on the surface, the country moved on as if nothing had occurred. The survivors could not complain or say anything about it; otherwise death would be their fate too. Death squads already existed in the 1970s.

Having escaped that massacre, my mother sought safety for me. She returned to the United States alone, seeking to obtain her permanent residency. Under U.S. Immigration laws in effect at that time, she was able to use the fact that I had been born in the United States to obtain residency. In 1965, President Johnson signed the Immigration and Nationality Act that made that possible. Former President John F. Kennedy and U.S. Senator Edward Kennedy were also instrumental in passing pro immigrant, landmark legislation that benefited millions of families.

My world of trees, birds, and nature's beauty disappeared on a fateful day in 1977. My grandpa had already passed away and my grandmother, aunts, and uncles did not want me to go back to the United States but my mother insisted. One day my mother appeared unannounced to bring me back to the United States. My aunt accompanied us to the bus station. From there, the two of us continued to San Salvador's airport.

I still remember being misled while they took me to the bus station at El Transito. I started crying and telling my aunt that she did not truly love me because she was allowing me to be taken away. I cried and cried and finally fell asleep. I'll never forget waking up and finding that I had accidentally busted my lip on the seat in front of me while I slept during the bus ride to the San Salvador airport.

I also recall getting on the airplane with my mother and asking why the plane did not move. Later on the flight, I had my first taste of 7-Up soda. I was fascinated by the little bubbles in the cup filled with 7-Up. It reminded me of the marbles that I used to play with in Usulutan– the ones that had little air bubbles. I was intrigued by these little air bubbles. Before I left San Salvador, I gave all of my marbles to my best friend Albertito, who had grown up with me in the town called Mejicanos, San Salvador. I told Albertito to keep my marbles so that when I returned we would play with them again. During the Civil War Albertito disappeared. Children were often forcefully recruited to fight in the war. Many were killed.

We finally landed at Los Angeles International Airport and an aunt picked us up. We first went to live with her on Crenshaw Boulevard near Wilshire. It was like a nightmare for me. I was enrolled at a local preschool where I cried every day as I could not understand or speak English. The teachers were not tolerant and sometimes mistreated me, because I did not stop crying. One day, one of the teachers placed tape on my mouth so I would stop crying. Adults can sometimes be inhumane and abusive toward helpless children. Not knowing that I was a U.S. born citizen of this country, the teachers even threatened to call "La Migra" (immigration agents) so they would take me away.

My aunt with whom we were staying was married to an Anglo senior citizen many years older than herself. She needed a "green card" and was definitely sacrificing to obtain her legal papers by living with Charles. He was a pack rat and a cheapskate. He wanted my aunt to eat rotten fruit and bathe in the same water he had used.

Sometimes Charles would walk me to preschool, but there were also days when I refused to go. He would speak to me in English that I could not understand. I barely recall that one day he tried to force me to stay at the preschool and I accidentally tore one of the buttons from his long sleeved shirt.

I hated that pre-school that had a picture of a clown and multi color balloons at the front door. That image did not mean happiness for me. I was so very much afraid of clowns, especially the ones that I remember from El Salvador. They would dress up in San Salvador and ride the buses saying practical jokes to get some spare change for their food. Instead of liking them or finding them funny, I thought that they were scary as hell.

While being forced to be at the preschool I would imagine flying away. Just like Superman. I even had a red jacket that with my imagination would help me fly away. But I was trapped and I knew that I was pretending—that it was a fantasy. I felt so much pain realizing that I was trapped in this preschool and with a new familia. I missed my grandmother's hugs and her coffee. I missed my favorite orange cup with a gold rim. I missed seeing her with her "delantar." I was her favorite and she used to spoil me. I was treated like a little prince by my family in Usulutan. I will never forget the image of my grandmother crying since she knew that I would leave her. She told me "te quiero mucho mi hijito" (I love you very much my little son).

Then I was in the United States with no protection or even knowing how to speak English. I missed being in the countryside and having the freedom to admire nature, climb trees to explore the little birds' eggs. I missed everything so very much and I felt so helpless and unprotected in Los Angeles.

Of course, my memories of El Salvador were those before the 1980s. As of 1980 the full bloodshed began to occur and the 12 year nightmare began—the cruel and inhumane Civil War. The Salvadoran Civil War (the nightmare) officially ended on January 16, 1992, through the signing of the Chapultepec Peace Accords in Mexico. During the 1970s, some violence was already occurring throughout El Salvador but the Civil War became official in 1980 when the five guerilla groups joined forces and officially declared war against the Salvadoran government. The dreaded nightmare began. The smell of blood and rotting, headless corpses would soon fill the roads and streets of this once beautiful country.

Chapter Two

The Dark Side

Even though my mother thought she had left the war behind, we soon found much violence in Los Angeles. After living on Crenshaw and Wilshire Blvd. for a couple of months, we soon had to relocate to 41st and Hoover Street in the now-infamous area known as South Central. These days that area is better known as South L.A., home of two of the largest gangs, The CRIPS and 18th Street gangs. One of my aunts lived there and she wanted us to become her neighbors.

We did not know that we were moving to the "Dark Side," so-named because of the high crime rate and the absence of street lights. It was literally like hell. During the night or dawn we could hardly see anything except what could be seen through the moon light. During the colder winters we could see thick fog and feel a bone chilling breeze.

Weeks after we moved there in 1979, a young Latino Cholo was shot while speaking on the phone. My mother ran across the street with a bottle of rubbing alcohol to give him First Aid. He was crying out in great despair for his mother, minutes later he died. I was six years old and in first grade. I could not fully comprehend what had occurred but everyone around me was shocked. Violence and disruption became routine in my neighborhood creating fear and confusion in our lives. These types of uncertain environments made young children face challenges that were not congruent with their ages. It either broke them down or made them tough. Most kids who live in violent neighborhoods adopt that survival attitude. Some kids in their early ages of life begin to say if "you mess with me then you are dead." Respect takes a different route—through violence and a tough ass attitude in order to survive.

My mother enrolled me at Menlo Avenue Elementary School under the name of Randy Jurado. That was my identity—the Jurado side, the Salvatrucha/guanaco side. Guanaco is used as a slang word for Salvadoran, it is meant

7

to be derogatory when used with the purpose to put someone down. But it can also be positive—as in guanaco pride. The Ertll side, my father's side, was not included since the secretary at Menlo Ave. did not bother to look at my name printed on my birth certificate. It was not until high school when a school district office clerk in Rochester, Minnesota cared to enroll me under my correct name. At Menlo, I was assigned to be in Ms. Bailoff's class. She was a veteran teacher and she was African American, as were 90% of the students in my class. Among the few Latinos, Cynthia and Ricky became my interpreters at times. And there was Mike Lee, the only Asian student in my class; he wanted to become a judge.

Luckily I was not crying every day now. I already had been kicked out of an elementary school on 76th Street and Figueroa for crying too much. Having no personal experience with deportation or discrimination based on language barriers, the teachers and principal could not understand my pain. Being accustomed to teaching only native speakers, they did not want to be disturbed by the demographic changes that were looming on the horizon.

Fortunately for me, I went from not being able to effectively communicate with the English speaking students in Ms. Bailoff's class to eventually speaking some English. I began to do well in math, and Ms. Bailoff was wonderful, encouraging me to do my best, even though one day she whacked my hand with a ruler after she saw me break three pencils. I was showing off for Cynthia by breaking pencils in halves. I had a crush on Cynthia, my first crush in elementary school. Ms. Bailoff, was the old school type of teacher. Ms Bailoff was a no, non-sense teacher and she was used to whacking students with rulers or a paddle. That is what I got for trying to impress the girls in my class.

Adjacent to the Los Angeles Coliseum and the University of Southern California, Menlo Avenue Elementary School was not an easy place for a recent immigrant to get used to. By second grade I was still struggling to learn how to read and write in Spanish and learning English at the same time. Typical of kids, I developed a crush on my second grade teacher, Ms. Tom, an Asian American lady. My first exposure to the Asian culture was in the mid 1970s when I watched the popular "Ultraman" Japanese show in El Salvador and also the Bruce Lee movies. As a small boy, I had dreams of wanting to become a great fighter like Bruce Lee.

My life took a turn for the better in third grade, when I was enrolled in Mr. Patrick O'Brien's classroom. He was a new teacher who had just moved from Washington State to Los Angeles. He was an Anglo bilingual teacher, with curly blonde hair; clearly of Irish descent. He knew of the struggles of immigrant kids and African Americans. He loved speaking Spanish, the Beatles, and camping. He still does.

He truly cared about the struggles and emotional pain of each student, whether Latino or African American, or any other race or ethnicity. He could relate because his ancestors lived during the Potato Famine in Ireland, when thousands of Irish died due to lack of food. I learned how to read and write in Spanish and English with Mr. O'Brien. He became a role model and family friend to this day. He believed in the great potential that each student has and he encouraged us to read and write. He selected me to be part of the gifted and talented program. Mr. O'Brien's classroom was a refuge for us. Being in the classrooms was more desirable than walking to our homes. The neighborhood had become a jungle or rather hell. Believe me, it was no "Leave It to Beaver" type of neighborhood. With Mr. O'Brien I learned that one teacher can definitely make a tremendous impact in the lives of thousands of students.

At the start of 4th grade my family moved to Huntington Park. I wanted to move to East Los Angeles, not South East. I had heard that some of the girls were prettier in East Los. It was a disaster and a painful experience to leave Menlo Avenue School and move to South East Los Angeles. We moved more than 30 times while I was a child, in search of tranquility and less violence. Things did not change much from place to place.

By the time we moved to Huntington Park, I started to notice differences among Latino groups. The variance was in immigration status, economic prosperity, culture, even language accents. Students from other Latino backgrounds began to make fun of my Salvadoran and African American-English linguistic rhythm. I would use "vos" instead of "tu," which translates to the English word meaning "you." I also looked different because of my French/Hungarian heritage from my father. I am proud of these roots but in Los Angeles, especially in South Central, it's rare to find French or Hungarian families. I had to adapt and I absorbed the cultures that were predominant in the neighborhoods where I lived. I only met one other Hungarian/Magyar kid during junior high school summer school.

Although I thought things would get better for me once that I learned English, my challenges were only increasing. I had a teacher named Ms. Jones at Malabar Elementary School in Huntington Park, who actually asked me if I had attended a school for dogs! Her question stemmed from the belief that I did not speak English correctly and I did not know how to do certain math problems. I still remember longing for another role model like Mr. O'Brien, but I was finding only teachers who were insensitive to the needs of low income children.

In 4th grade the meaning of graffiti still eluded me. Along Florence Avenue, I kept seeing "F13," which was an abbreviation for Florencia 13. I knew this was different than what I had seen in South Central, which was usually a reference to the 18th Street Gang. But I really did not understand any of it: I really did not know what it meant until 5th or 6th grade, when some of my classmates started joining gangs or getting jumped in (beaten) in order to belong.

My family decided to move back to South Central and live near 41st and Hoover. I returned to Menlo and was placed in Mr. O'Brien's fourth grade class. I was in heaven again. Now we would sing Christmas carols during the holidays and serenade the students in all the other classes. I felt protected in Mr. O'Brien's class, even though the streets were hell and I was surrounded by violence, day and night.

One of my best friends, Miguel, was an immigrant whose ten year old brother, Luis, was beaten one day in the Menlo Avenue playground by another student for refusing to give him gum. That very day, Luis decided to be jumped into the 18th Street Gang. Years later I learned that he was in prison for life.

I began to notice how many of the young men were either shot dead by other gang members or were prosecuted and sent to prison for decades or for life. The juvenile system and prison system do not improve the human quality of these young men and women. Many of the young men and women report incidents of being beaten and raped in prison. Despite everything, I still believe that our youth should be given an opportunity to improve their lives and become productive members in society. It is a known reality that when someone comes out of jail, it is difficult to reintegrate into society and rehabilitation is unaffordable for many of them. Many ex prisoners get out of jail seeking revenge, which leads to high levels of crime and violence. They want revenge for the physical and sexual abuse that they experienced in prison. Sometimes other gang members pay the price and sometimes innocent victims pay the price when revenge takes place.

By the time I reached 5th grade, Mexican students were no longer the only recent immigrant group from a Spanish speaking background. A large number of Central American immigrants (Salvadoran, Guatemalan, Nicaraguan, Belizean, and Honduran) were now residing in the South Los Angeles area. I began to meet kids who had just arrived from El Salvador and Guatemala at Menlo and the surrounding community. Most were shy and timid children who had already witnessed brutality first hand.

My best friend at the time was an African American kid named Mark. He was half African American and half Mexican. He identified with both cultures, and his father was kind to cook breakfast for us. These days, I wonder what happened to Mark. We watched out for each other. We had adventures of innocent children who liked to play video games, buy hamburgers, and walk around South Central. Mark and I became *bodyguards* for a Mexican senior citizen. We accompanied and protected him while he sold oranges throughout South Central. This was our first job: He would buy us lunch at Kentucky Fried Chicken and give us quarters to play video games. The last time that I saw the older gentleman was when we were moving to Huntington Park. I still remember his watery eyes, filled with tears when he came to pick me up and realized that I was moving. I never saw this street vendor again. Later on, I eventually lost touch with my friend Mark. I looked for him after we all left elementary school, and never found him. But I did learn that he was eventually recruited into the new gang in the neighborhood, Street Villains and then his family moved to the Valley where he joined another gang.

Mark was the first of my close friends to get lost, and many others followed. While drifting away from childhood friends is not unusual anywhere, this was different. I was losing my friends to the world of gangs, a world far apart from the world of focusing on academics.

Among the recent immigrants from El Salvador and Guatemala was Armando, a small, hulk-like boy from Guatemala who became my best friend. His voice was deep for his age and boy did the other kids make fun of him with so much cruelty. What the other kids did not know was that even though he was just 10 years old, the Guatemalan civil war had hardened Armando. He had seen how the indigenous Mayas were rounded up and exterminated in various villages by the military and the Patrullas de Auto Defensa Civil— PAC (The Civil Defense Patrols).

Armando was so poor that when we were about to graduate from sixth grade, he realized he did not have the proper clothes and did not want to attend the graduation. I let him wear some of my clothes. We sang "The World is a Rainbow" and "We Are the World" for our graduation. It wasn't a rainbow when children were recruited to become hard-core gangsters in elementary school. The Los Angeles Unified School District (LAUSD) was faced with a large number of immigrant students from varying backgrounds and socio-political experiences. These students required special transitional programs, which did not really exist. LAUSD administrators and teachers were caught off guard with the wave of immigrant children that enrolled in public schools throughout the 1980s. Some of these teachers and administrators were not prepared for advocating or for providing a quality education for immigrant children.

Armando survived being picked on and beaten by gang members. Although he was disliked just because of how he dressed, he was not intimidated at all. He stood up to the bullies, especially "big Robert" from 18th Street, who was a giant even back in elementary school. Way back then, he was already doing power lifting, and playing soccer with adults. He was simply the school bully and preyed on the smaller and weaker kids. This other guy named Miguel was his crony who would usually pick on poor Armando too. But Armando would not back down.

In sixth grade, I served as interpreter for the parents when they came to school to speak to our teacher, Ms. Arnold. They wanted to know why their children were changing; why they were becoming cholos and cholas (gang members). Often reduced to tears, they wanted to save their children. But the streets were more alluring and powerful than the parents or the public school system.

Some of these children were abused in their own homes. Some were abused at school, too. It's no wonder they felt that they needed to escape by joining a gang. Many had grown up in households full of domestic violence. They saw savagery and brutality. Unfortunately plenty of them began to copy this behavior. Guns were becoming part of the scene in the neighborhood and a lot of kids wanted to own one for protection. Some young men and women were turned on by the smell of the gun powder and felt empowered—would get a high when they would participate in drive by shootings. Since that era, the rivalries and the calibers of guns have only grown larger. Some of these young girls and boys did not realize what they were getting into. They soon found out by directly getting involved in violence. Their innocence soon vanished and they no longer feared authority or their gang rivals. Most took a loyalty oath that they would die to defend their gang, their so-called familia. Many realized that they would not live very long. Many had lost any type of hope or empathy towards others. Especially, the young girls who were gang raped as a ritual to join the gang.

The cement streets of Los Angeles absorbed blood from gang-related violence then, and they continue to absorb blood from gang related violence now.

Let's hope that the Superintendent and School Board members of the Los Angeles Unified School District (LAUSD) will begin to improve public education for all children. Especially in the poor areas of Los Angeles that continue to be neglected and ignored.

Chapter Three

Can African Americans and Latinos Get Along?

Entering James A. Foshay Junior High School in 1985 was like entering Corcoran, Pelican Bay or the County Jail. The fences were huge, and the school had to hire security guards to maintain control over the student population. At times, control seemed elusive.

Some students would beat up teachers or even the principal. Some teachers developed romantic and sexual relationships with under-age students. It left many students feeling lost and unprotected both at home and at school.

One teacher, in particular, developed such strong ties with the students that she kept in touch with them and she would visit the one's that would end up in prison for life. Some of these young men eventually became members of the Mexican Mafia. They "green lighted" that teacher and put out a hit on her since she knew too much and could serve as a potential witness. She had no choice but to go into the witness protection program.

Armando was immediately drawn to the gang life and was recruited to join the newly formed Mara Salvatrucha (MS 13). Fed up with being picked on and beaten by the Mexican American and African American students, he found refuge through violence.

Our innocence was slowly destroyed by the bloody sidewalks. We were easy prey since we were small kids compared to the hard-core gangsters who had already committed murders and felonies. They were 20 plus year old adults picking on 12, 13, 14, and 15 year old kids.

We would walk the streets like child soldiers, taking refuge in our books and tennis shoes. But we had to learn not to run from the attacks and robberies. We learned to be brave—to stand up and defend ourselves. I was suspended twice for getting into bloody fights at school; I had to defend myself. Either you choose to defend yourself or you get punked, picked on every day. We learned that we had to develop a reputation of being chingones

13

(bad asses) or in good Salvadoran slang—truchas. Vergones (the tough ones). This was no environment for the weak and meek. You eventually began to model—to copy others—just to survive.

One memory is still vivid in my mind. When Armando and I were walking along Exposition Street, an African-American gang member yanked off Armando's gold chain, which held a cross given to him by his parents. Those injustices tore into the soul. In time, the scars on the outside would shrink, but his anger and rage grew. One day, Armando was stabbed in front of me. It was very hard to see him bleeding. I watched him bleed, feeling frustrated since there was not much that I could do since I would have also gotten stabbed. I felt guilty—but I later realized that it was not my fault since Armando had made his own choices in life and no one at that time could stop the violent rampage. Also, he had written his gang (MS 13) on his pants that made him stand-out and he became an immediate target for his rivals—Harpys/Dead End/ Mid City Stoners. Armando swore that no one would ever pick on him and he chose to establish a close relationship with the Eighteenth Street gang. They were much bigger then—and they were known to take care of business. Initially, 18th Street was the biggest and most violent gang in the early 1980s. Armando went to them and he got back up. The guys that stabbed Armando got a taste of their own medicine. Armando chose to use machetes and AK 47s to take revenge. I eventually lost touch with Armando, but I always considered him a friend and tried to help him—but he made his own decisions to survive.

The gangster life involves jumping people and protecting one's neighborhoods. Street law has no boundaries and respect is interpreted in peculiar ways. You learn not to stare too long at someone or it is considered disrespect. You can get shot.

The common question before being shot or stabbed is "Where you from?" How you answer can determine whether you are shot, stabbed or allowed to go your own way. They're not asking what country, city or state. . . . It means, "What street gang are you from?" Some kids who don't fully speak English may respond innocently by naming the street they live on, and then paying with their lives.

The gangster life comes at you from all directions. I met a girl who became my girlfriend when I was in seventh grade. She was from the 18th Street gang and I did not have a complete picture of what she was involved in. Even though I was growing up in this environment, I still was somewhat naïve and innocent. At age 14 she was already drinking, smoking, and doing other illegal stuff. Under that tough attitude, she was a little girl who was a fan of Cindy Lauper, the 1980s pop star that sang "Girls Just Wanna Fun."

After we broke up, I never saw her again but I still remember that she kept my school I.D.. I sometimes wonder if she decided to turn her life around.

Overall, I am glad our time together was short lived and that I did not get shot for being with a cholita (female gangster). She sort of wanted to stop and reform, but was too deep into the gangster lifestyle and she eventually learned to like it.

What is truly sad is that many innocent victims in South Central are murdered. These killings go uncounted and untold. It is still taboo to talk about the unresolved murders. Witnesses cannot testify, if they did, there will be repercussions.

The 1980s was a decade of crack-cocaine, gang wars, and police brutality in South LA. Mayor Tom Bradley kept stating and behaving as if everything was all right, when in fact most things were not right—at least not in lower-income areas. Of course, it may well have been all right for the people living in nice, quiet, well protected neighborhoods. The story of the two Los Angeles has not changed much since the Bradley administration. The rich Los Angeles and the poor Los Angeles—even though we have our Latino Mayor, Antonio Villaraigosa. He is trying to bridge that gap.

Poor minorities went on being innocent victims of drive-bys, armed robberies, beatings, and murder. Those who suffered the most were the recent immigrants, who were beaten by both the police and gang members. They were scared to report crimes because they feared they would be deported or accused of the crimes. Unable to speak English, they had no way to defend themselves.

There's no question that some "ethnic attacks" did take place. Even to this day, we want to hide and deny those facts. I was in 5th grade when I witnessed the beating of an African American man who was robbing a van. He was captured by some old veterano Latino Cholos and beaten to death. I was a young kid and I wondered about such brutality and inhumanity. I had seen the police beat individuals in my community, but I had never seen such brutality perpetrated by civilians. The seeds of further violence and hatred were being planted by irresponsible adults, who taught children to hate those from other ethnic groups.

African-Americans and Latinos have more issues in common, than not. Both communities face high unemployment rates, high dropout rates, systemic poverty, gang violence, a disproportionate number of prison inmates and continual discrimination. Therefore, it is in the best interest of both communities to form coalitions focused on common issues that need to be tackled and resolved together. That was the philosophy that I learned from the former Executive Director of the Coalition for Humane Immigrant Rights (CHIRLA), Luke Williams. He is African American but he is fully bilingual and actually lived in El Salvador. He has been a champion in advocating for African American and Latinos to get along and respect each other.

We need to do more to accentuate the history of alliances between African-Americans and Latinos. We must remember the humane role Mexicans played with the underground railroad during slavery. Creating a southern route, Mexicans enabled an estimated 10,000 escaped slaves to arrive in freedom south of the border.

However, we must be realistic. Building effective communication, alliances, and working relationships between African American and Latinos is not an easy task that will be accomplished in a few years. It will take decades of constant work for both communities to continue learning more about each other's history, culture, and further respect each other.

Some progress has been made, but we have a long way to go. President Barack Obama can in fact help to bring both communities to work together on common issues, to develop more respect and trust, which will benefit our society.

Chapter Four

A Better Chance Program

I wanted to escape this hell, so I applied to A Better Chance, a program established in 1963 to mainly help African-American students who lived in the inner city. Oprah Winfrey and singer Diana Ross are strong supporters of the ABC program. Oprah has donated over $12 million to the program.

I had learned about A Better Chance when Michael Anderson, an official from the University of Southern California and a recruiter for the program, came to Foshay Junior High School to give a presentation. Students who showed academic and leadership potential were encouraged to apply.

I was one of the few Latino students who attended the orientation session, along with some of the other so-called bright students. I applied and was initially rejected by Deerfield Academy in Massachusetts. I felt crushed. I wrote to the ABC headquarters and pleaded with them to please "save me." Two weeks after I started attending Jefferson High School, I received a call informing me that a slot was open at a school in Rochester, Minnesota. I had already half convinced myself that Jefferson was not too bad—even though murders were common in the surrounding neighborhood and violence was rampant on campus. These were the 1980s.

The person who called me with the great news was Anna McGee - a member of the Rochester National Association for the Advancement of Colored People (NAACP). I remember how happy I felt to learn the good news. I knew this was my chance to escape all the violence and chaos that made it so hard to focus on reading, writing, and learning. I had developed a deep, natural curiosity for knowledge, but the public schools were set up as prison preparatories. Where I grew up, you had two choices: you joined either a gang or the police department.

While in junior high school, I had chosen to become an LAPD Explorer at Southwest Police Station. I excelled and even won the station trophy for excellent area recruit. However, at the academy for LAPD Explorers, I had a life changing experience when one of the LAPD training officers pulled my hair because I had not heard him tell me to move out of the way. That incident deflated my interest in becoming a law enforcement officer. I concluded early on that we were not protected by the gangs or the rogue police officers who took advantage of their badge. Power can indeed corrupt certain individuals. It's interesting to further analyze the reasons why poor, minority kids from the inner city, grow up with a fear and distrust of the police. One of the strongest reasons has been the historical police brutality against minorities in areas such as South Central. It's simple, they do not have the economic clout or political connections to denounce or take effective legal steps to prevent or obtain true justice when police brutality occurs. Many times, the victims are intimidated not just by the gang members but also police officers who have beaten them. They are afraid to press charges or testify in court since repercussions and retaliation is common in poor neglected neighborhoods. Set ups are not uncommon.

South Central Los Angeles and Rochester, Minnesota are two completely different worlds. Rochester, Minnesota is known to be a safe and affluent city. It is basically a white, Midwestern world where the world famous IBM and Mayo Clinic are located.

At first I did not fit in Minnesota, but I slowly became friends with my African American housemates and the white students at school. I slowly learned to get to know and trust white people. I had never been truly exposed to them in South Central, except for Mr. O'Brien. But he had been one of us all along. I also had some superficial exposure to the USC white students and Raiders fans that would come to see the games at the Coliseum and park in the poor neighborhoods for a cheaper price. When the games or concerts were over, the fans would leave tons of trash on the streets and on the sidewalks of the poor neighborhoods. They were never cited by the police for littering.

When I had just arrived in Rochester it was hard, because the African American students at the Rochester house bonded and united. My first year I felt like an outcast because the only other Latino student in the Rochester Better Chance program was too reserved to take an interest in being my friend or mentor. He would avoid speaking to me at John Marshall High School. He had been in Rochester a long time, so he saw himself as part of the white world, and was not so eager to associate himself with another Latino. It hurt that he was not willing to help a younger kid. But his bitterness was something I would eventually come to understand.

When certain people endure pain, they often struggle to keep the bitterness at bay and they desperately want to "fit in" and be accepted by the majority. However, it is sad that some minorities desperately want to assimilate and they try to give up their own cultural roots to be accepted among the majority. Sometimes they will be partly accepted and used to mistreat their own community. They start to believe that they are better than the recent immigrants. A common phrase used in the 1970s Chicano movement to describe these type of individuals was "el vendido." The sell out. Sometimes they refer to them by the nickname of "coconut"—brown on the outside and white in the inside.

I knew I had to survive on my own and not rely on anyone. That's how it had always been. I had been trying to protect my mother, my two sisters, and myself. Life would have been great if someone had protected me, but that wasn't in the cards. That is how thousands of poor inner city kids survive. Through self-protection.

Many kids who grew up in the inner city and in war zones have undiagnosed cases of Post Traumatic Stress Disorder. Other "urban soldiers" get pushed over the edge by drugs and violence. I decided to take a different route by applying to the A Better Chance program. I began to excel in my classes in Rochester, MN. I lifted weights and joined the wrestling team and I soon learned that it is one of the toughest sports in the world. Ironically, while growing up in South Central I had been obsessed with the legendary Mexican wrestler "El Santo" (The Saint). I wanted to become a wrestler so that I would one day take the mask off the Mil Mascaras wrestler (Thousand Masks) or El Santo. I literally had dreams about me wrestling in the World Wrestling Federation. The French wrestler, Andre the Giant, was also my other wrestling hero. Once I joined the wrestling team in Rochester, MN, I soon realized that it was no joke or acting - wrestling is a serious sport in the Midwest, especially in Iowa. By learning to become tougher through wrestling, I began to obtain more confidence that I could do well in high school. I began to believe more in myself and that I could succeed and help my family. I was finally in an environment without violence and abuse. I could focus on studying in Rochester, MN and not worry about getting shot.

Lee Shibley was our live-in tutor. He was a physical therapist at the world-famous Mayo Clinic. To this day, I respect and admire Lee. He became like my big brother. Physically very large, he also had an incredible IQ. I learned so much from him and he being white was irrelevant to the friendship and trust that we built with each other. Lee taught me to believe in myself and to academically not give up. He would stay late into the evening helping me with my science, math, and writing projects. He taught me how to visualize and how to achieve my goals. He would even take the time to take me to the gym with him to work out. He showed me that he truly cared through actions and not just words.

Larry and Lou Kayner were my house parents, and to me, they were like real parents. Lou taught me about tough love and did not allow me to be sad or make excuses for not succeeding. Larry would take me to Wendy's restaurant every Saturday, and we would eat hamburger combos. We would have small talks—but meaningful ones. I got to know Larry's real soul and his struggle of being a lifelong truck driver, being a devout Christian, and how the banks had taken away everything that he owned—they took part of his soul. Larry hated the banks for what they had done to his life and family. He missed a couple of mortgage payments and the bank repossessed his home in Michigan. He never trusted banks again. Unfortunately, during my senior year in high school Larry passed away due to several illnesses and a few years later Lou died from cancer. Larry passed away on my birthday and I will never forget his kind soul.

I learned a great deal from Larry and Lou, and from others who served as my host families for Sundays. I learned that white people also face similar, if not, the same struggles that Latinos and African Americans face on a daily basis. They strive to provide to their families and to try to secure a stable future for their children. My Sunday host families included Wayne Larson (an engineer at IBM) and Kitty Larson (a school teacher); Brenda Dicken (a town council representative) and Charles Dicken (a dermatologist at Mayo Clinic). These people taught me how to study and be focused. Dr. Dicken even included me in the "doctoral residency" program that he supervised. I was able to perform surgeries on guinea pigs. My host families believed in me. They were kind individuals who wanted to help minority kids to succeed and they opened their homes and hearts to us.

I struggled to fit in at Rochester and made the best of it and focused on studying. Of course, I always ran into ignorant teachers who believed that minorities could not learn. I disliked Mr. Smith, who taught computer programming, because he always referred to me as "Jose." I did not do well in that class because I would skip it to go lift weights. Why would I want to learn from an ignorant teacher who clearly did not like Latinos?

Luckily, I still maintained good grades and applied to Occidental College and Whittier College. I was accepted to both, but I decided to attend "Oxy" because somehow I could never find Whittier College when my friend Danny and I went to visit. In retrospect, I am glad that we got lost on the freeway when we were heading to visit Whittier College. We never found it; therefore I chose to attend Occidental. It is interesting to note that our former President Richard Nixon attended Whittier College and President Barack Obama attended Occidental College.

Danny does not know it, but years earlier, he had convinced me to join the LAPD Explorers. He grew up in East L.A. among the "White Fence" and "Maravilla" gangsters. His father had been an OG (original gangster) from Maravilla. But his dad used to beat and mistreat Danny. He never told me but I knew, even though his dad had already passed away. Danny was a young man who had suffered a lot but he had a big heart. He always came to my house to pick me up and he would shout, "Jurado, let's go. It's time to go to the Academy!" It was tough to leave my best friends when I left for Rochester, MN when I was only 15 years old. A skinny kid who still wore t-shirts and Dickies pants. I had adopted the way my friends dressed in my community and school. I did not realize or know about "profiling." I merely thought that it was normal to dress that way—that it was "suave" or cool.

I missed all of my friends so very much when I went to Rochester. When I came back to visit during the summers, I would attend Manual Arts High School, just to get the feel of being in a local high school. And I would spend time with Danny: He would pick me up every Saturday morning.

A major influence in my life, Danny was kind of crazy and his dream was to become a police officer. He was excited about it. Danny was a Chicano in South Central. He was a transplant from East L.A. and I liked it. We became great friends since we had many things in common. We cared about our families especially because our neighborhood environment was hell. We wanted to improve our neighborhood.

One summer, I looked for Danny and found him in the hospital with bandages around his head. He said he was sick. He never told me that a Latino LAPD police officer had beaten him to the point of injuring his brain. He was accused of trying to steal a car when he was merely sleeping in a car with his brother. He had not been allowed to stay home that night since his mom was having an affair with a younger man. When the officers arrived, they mistreated his younger brother and Danny intervened and was beaten.

He was charged with a felony and was never able to achieve his dream of becoming a police officer. It was heartbreaking, because he admired and respected police officers so much. I lost touch with Danny, so I fall back on memories. Memories of young kids who thought we could make a difference, while adults kept destroying our dreams and ignoring our potential. I often wish my elementary school friends could have chosen a better future for themselves.

There was one positive development during my time at Foshay Junior High School. I met Antonio in seventh grade. He was a young Mexican immigrant who loved to play with Transformers. He became my best friend and remains so to this day. He is extremely intelligent and a caring person. Out of darkness comes some hope. We still see each other and we still compete to see who can bench press the most. When close friends are like family, nationality loses its importance. When we get together, we are simply human and we share love and memories of a cruel past. Antonio taught me about Pedro Infante—the famous Mexican singer who died in an airplane crash. Interestingly, Pedro Infante's best friend was from El Salvador since he liked to fly to visit El Salvador from Mexico.

Before leaving to Rochester, MN I had gotten my first official job was when I was 14 years old. An Italian American named Richard Godino and Toni O'Donnell hired me that summer to work for the City of Los Angeles Recreation and Parks Department. I was a locker attendant at Exposition Park's Swim Stadium pool.

Both my job at the pool and my experience during junior high school as an LAPD Explorer taught me how to be disciplined and how to conduct myself in a war zone. To avoid the bullets.

I was somewhat safe at the Swim Stadium since the violence was contained in certain spots in the area. Since I had grown up around there, the local gang members already knew who I was. Unfortunately, I also ended up working at South Park pool on 52nd and Avalon Street in the heart of South Los Angeles. It was no walk in the park working there in the late 1980s. Homicides, prostitution, and drug dealing were rampant. South Park was no joke. If you survived working there—you earned stripes and your colleagues would refer to you as a survivor or veteran of war. I earned my stripes while working there—in a serious way.

One day while I was wearing my LAPD Explorer shirt from Newton Station I was jumped and hit on the face by an ex-convict who had just gotten out of the County Jail and hated cops. I was too young to realize that cops were not welcomed or liked in that area of town. I was blessed to not have been shot or stabbed that day. The convict had just been released and he did not have a weapon. Such individuals seek out victims and they get so much joy from attacking or murdering others. They are pathological murderers.

These types of injustices created much anger in me. I was sick and tired of seeing innocent victims robbed or shot.

A few years later while I was in the A Better Chance program I had an incredible experience that helped me cope with my nightmares and bottled up anger. I was awarded a scholarship to attend the Outward Bound program in the Blue Ridge Mountains of North Carolina. My high school counselor, Mr. Espinda, was instrumental in helping me learn about this program.

I took city clothes and construction boots. I did not know what to wear or what kind of shoes to take. I had no idea that we were going to be hiking, rock climbing, white water canoeing, and surviving under pouring rain for three consecutive weeks. It was the most horrible, yet wonderful experience in my life.

I met some truly disturbed young boys and girls from all over the United States. Some had tried to commit suicide, one of them was a white supremacist supporter, and others had horrible problems at home. I was surprised to find that I considered myself o.k. in comparison to them. And I thought that South Central was crazy.

While being stuck in the Blue Ridge Mountains I was tormented by the fact that I had left my family alone in Los Angeles. I felt that my mother and sisters needed me and one day I just broke down since I knew that my family needed me for protection. I felt that I had left my family alone and felt tremendous guilt. I still picture my little sister crying for me when I would get dropped off at the airport. She would plead for me not to leave. While I was in the Blue Ridge Mountains I could not wait to return to Los Angeles. Nevertheless, once the airplane landed back in Los Angeles, I was a more mature person. I was more responsible and had a better perspective about life. I felt that I could conquer the world and that I could help change my community. Those three weeks in the Blue Ridge Mountains taught me to survive in the natural environment and to get to know myself. I began to understand why I was angry, so furious, and why I had insomnia. I always feared for my life. I had grown up that way. Have you ever wondered how individuals live in a war zone?

The guerrillas, the military or the death squads were always after you in El Salvador. Whether you were guilty or not. All it took was a rumor or gossiper who wanted to get rid of someone they did not like. Many innocent civilians and children were murdered due to lying, evil tongues. Someone would accuse campesinos (farmers/peasants) of being subversives to justify killing them and stealing their land. Most of the campesinos were honest, hard working, and extremely religious people. They were humble and upright in their moral believes.

Many Salvadorans refugees barely escaped being murdered. While in Rochester, Minnesota I met many Salvadoran and Nicaraguan refugees who were temporarily living at Assisi Heights (The Sisters of Saint Francis of Rochester, MN). This is a huge religious order for Catholic Roman nuns. Assisi Heights is located on a hill top in an extraordinary building near John Marshall High School. Central American refugees were brought to work and live there before they would request political asylum into Canada. I became really good friends with a Nicaraguan refugee kid who was attending high school at John Marshall HS. He told me how he had been recruited to fight in the war and how they would mistreat him. I still remember the faces of the refugees. The war had created a look of fear and distrust—of anguish and pain. They had witnessed atrocities.

During the Salvadoran Civil War many betrayals took place, therefore many people lost trust and hope. Envy and jealousy led to many false accusations and death of innocent civilians. Some members of the wealthy families were kidnapped for ransom money. Some were murdered. Kidnappings became a big business during the Civil War.

In Los Angeles, either the gangs or the police were after kids who supposedly fit the "profile." In the 1980s, 1990s and even now, young people continue to feel unsafe in South LA since they are stereotyped as being thugs or gang members, when many times they are not.

Chapter Five

Occidental College Years

Attending Occidental College was an intellectual journey. One reason I chose Occidental was because of its focus on multicultural education. I was also thrilled with the generous partial scholarship they offered me. I did also obtain student loans in order to pay for my education.

Oxy was indeed a hidden utopia. Barack Obama attended from 1979 to 1981 before transferring to Columbia University. We have great hopes that President Obama will improve our inner cities. I hope that he will help reduce the number of poor people who get incarcerated since most cannot afford to obtain competent and caring legal representation. During President Obama's two years at Oxy, he was already forming his political philosophy. He was opposed to the Apartheid system in South Africa and he was concerned with the violence in Central America.

At Oxy, I realized that Latinos, as a community, do have their own needs, including immigration reform and bilingual education.

The bread-and-butter issues that affect Latinos and blacks also affect low-income and middle income whites. After all, most community members simply seek to have affordable housing, secure jobs, health insurance, enough money to feed and educate their children, and Social Security and Medicare benefits for retirement.

These are issues that impact everyone, not just ethnic community members. I learned about these concepts and also about the philosophy of a multicultural society through the Multicultural Summer Institute (MSI) that I attended at Occidental College in 1991.

Oxy was a place of ideas, concepts, books, writing papers, and having philosophical conversations with other students. I would spend all nighters debating life and social issues with my roommates Matthew Herrick from New York and Donald Sanchez from New Mexico. Many, if not most of the Oxy students, came from upper middle class and wealthy families from throughout the United States. This made it even more interesting, because poor, middle class, and wealthy people learned together and participated in heated debates and discussions.

At parties and in terms of the social scene, I discovered the "Rock En Espanol" mania while I was at Oxy. I began to listen to Mana, Caifanes, Miguel Mateos, Heroes del Silencio, La Ley, Enanitos Verdes, and others. On the weekends, I became immersed in this world with friends from my old neighborhoods. It was my escape from just focusing on academia and student activism. I was also able to observe first-hand the high rate of alcoholism that exists in the Latino community and how this has become an epidemic. It made more sense to see how certain holidays such as "Cinco de Mayo" were and are still promoted through sponsorships and advertising from the alcohol industry. Many youth see commercials that show beautiful women being attracted to men who are drinking various brands of beers or hard liquor. These are the lessons that you learn on the streets and in the dance clubs where you are not judged by your intelligence but by your looks.

At Occidental, I learned a great deal about ethnic minority history and politics, European philosophy, and the struggles of Latin American countries. I learned about the role the United States has played in our global society in the diplomacy and world affairs courses that I took. I learned about African American, Latino, Asian, Jewish, gay and lesbian issues. Oxy's African American president, Dr. John Brooks Slaughter, took risks by trying to diversify the ethnic makeup of the school's student population. He even recruited some top-notch minority professors. Dr. Slaughter was innovative and he did make many people upset and uncomfortable due to his worldview of a multicultural society and that he pushed the envelope by allowing taboo issues to be taught within the classroom. Eventually Dr. Slaughter moved on but he made a remarkable difference by implementing academic rigor with a multicultural vision. He was ahead of his time. We now know that President Barack Obama was able to also promote multiculturalism as a key to developing a multi ethnic coalition that helped him win his election.

Oxy was a place to be challenged intellectually, but I also knew far too well the harsh realities of where I came from. I did expand my knowledge and I learned to question why certain injustices existed while taking courses with Professor Peter Dreier and Professor Manuel Pastor. I began to understand the history of Los Angeles; the different political struggles and the injustices such as the infamous "Zoot Suit Riots" of the 1940s. I learned about the Black Panthers and about the United Nations, and about economic inequities.

I learned about the struggle of Justice for Janitors through the leadership of Maria Elena Durazo. I found out that many of the rank and file leaders of this movement were Salvadorans. They already knew about union organizing from their home country. They were seasoned organizers.

I began to see the role that city hall plays and how the resources are distributed throughout the City of Los Angeles. I saw how South L.A. had been and still is purposely ignored and neglected by our elected officials.

I obtained the "McKelvey Reath Fellowship" and worked at City Hall with Councilmember Mike Hernandez. The other fellows and I were so proud that he was an Oxy alumnus who had used intelligence and determination to climb the political ladder.

I learned what power can do to people. It can build you up or destroy you. Politicians have to decide whether to improve their communities or to increase their personal gains. I was able to observe how people gravitate and kiss up to people in power, but will purposely ignore people they see as powerless or useless. I also learned about the United Farm Workers, Concerned Citizens of South Central, Mothers of East Los Angeles, and the history of the Salvadoran Civil War and the Mexican Revolution.

Everything started to make sense and I wanted to apply the theoretical knowledge in my South Central neighborhood. I started to believe that I could make a difference; I was a motivated young man. I started to organize my community members, African American and Latino, in an effort to decrease the violence in South Central. It was not easy. But it was better than doing nothing at all. Most people, even pastors and priests, had already given up. I did not want to become apathetic and disillusioned. I admire those who did not give up, and they taught me to have hope and faith. There are pastors and priests who truly care and are making a difference in their own communities. Most, in fact, are making a significant difference and they need to be recognized and applauded.

I still wanted to make a difference, so I did an internship with the Central American Resource Center (CARECEN) while at Occidental College. I became proud of my roots. I began to eat more pupusas—instead of just hamburgers. But I soon realized that "ethnic foods" do not determine your identity. I started to tell other students that it was more important for students to read about their own history than just having parties where alcohol was served with ethnic food. I was becoming more politicized and conscious of different social issues.

I started to meet different activists and I began to help them to get Temporary Protective Status (TPS) granted for Central American immigrants. We began to support the struggle for the Nicaraguan and Central American Adjustment Act (NACARA). Permanent residency had been granted to Nicaraguans, but Salvadorans, Hondurans, and Guatemalans were excluded, so we tried to address this imbalance.

The combined effort of the Salvadoran government, through the effective leadership of Salvadoran Ambassador Rene Leon, and U.S. Salvadoran community-based organizations led to Temporary Protected Status being granted. Central American community groups and the Salvadoran consulates throughout the United States have limited resources to help so many people with immigration legal issues. Fraud by public notaries and other unscrupulous entities that are so-called legal advisors take advantage. I learned about this while I did my internship at CARECEN. Families would come crying, saying that they had received notices of deportation after a fraudulent public notary misled them.

Unscrupulous individuals have a history of feeding off immigrant groups, and misleading them. Exploiters overcharge and commonly promise TPS eligible applicants permanent legal status - something they cannot provide.

The U.S. government should adopt a policy of zero tolerance in dealing with such individuals. But, it takes time to catch and prosecute those who perpetrate these frauds and destroy the lives of innocent families by their greed and incompetence.

Community groups have a long record of serving the immigrant community. Immigrants must become better informed to seek out organizations that charge reasonable fees and provide quality legal services. Let's face the fact that some organizations have more credibility among community members.

Sadly for our community, TPS is a temporary status and a temporary solution. As one deadline passes, another looms. And the fears of our people are constant that they will be deported sooner or later, once TPS expires. A concrete and humane solution needs to be found by President Barack Obama and Congress.

TPS applicants are hard-working, tax-paying and law-abiding. The U.S. government has already identified them. Legislatively, it is feasible to grant them the opportunity to become permanent residents of the United States.

TPS has greatly benefited tens of thousands of Salvadorans and Hondurans nationwide. It has contributed directly toward the gradual rebuilding of El Salvador's infrastructure that was devastated by the two earthquakes in 2001 and Hurricane Mitch. Through remittances of more than $2.5 billion annually, TPS refugees have helped keep the Salvadoran economy afloat. In a tangible manner, it has helped Salvadorans both in the United States and in our homeland.

It is time to end the anxieties of those who have contributed so greatly to its success and to offer them a chance to become full partners in a country they have come to know and love as their new home. Advocating for approval of TPS was one of my first full immersions in policy advocacy. It was also personal; I wanted my uncle to obtain his permanent residency. He is a kind soul who had always told us stories back in El Salvador and in the United States he always took me to the movies when I was child. We would listen to music together from the European group Modern Talking and The Beatles. He always used to role play El Chapulin Colorado (a famous Mexican comedy character from the show El Chespirito) and he would say "siganme los buenos" (the good ones, follow me). My uncle was a mentor to me.

I began to read more about my own history and in my first year at Oxy, I joined MEChA/ALAS (Movimiento Estudiantil Chicano de Aztlan / Association of Latin American Students) and I was even elected Secretary. Under this position I learned more about the Chicano struggle and La Causa (The Cause). I also began to wonder about the Centroamericano struggle and its history. Thus in my second year at Oxy I was thoroughly influenced by a history course that I took with Professor Margaret Crahan, "Coming of Crisis in Latin America."

I began to see how the Salvadoran, Guatemalan, Honduran, and Nicaraguan people had suffered many injustices. They had endured tragedies, robberies, rapes, and murders in their own home countries, only to relive those same nightmares while crossing Mexico as "undocumented immigrants." Then they arrived in the United States to face more discrimination and hatred at the workplace, schools, and neighborhoods.

I began to understand the roots and causes of violence. When I learned that the little kids at Menlo and Foshay had been guerrillas and boy soldiers in their home countries. They knew how to put together guns like AK 47s, M-16s, and how to build other kinds of weapons. They knew how to use *machetes* since they grew up on farms, where massive trees and plants were cut. Most children recruits were taken by force and taught to become merciless killers.

Subsequently, a few young Salvadoran kids decided to form their own gang and that it spread like wild fire. Soon it was a notorious gang, imitating and surpassing Chicano and African American gangs in terms of homicides. They were not messing around.

They became known as the "Mara Salvatruchas" (MS 13). Their heavy metal music and style of dress were influenced by satanic messages. They were like real rockers with an attitude and at first they did not look like Cholos. Many dressed in black and considered themselves "stoners"—rockers/heavy metal fans. But they eventually adopted the Cholo look. Even one of its founders, who is now dead, stated that they opened the door and allowed the devil to enter. He repented about the gang life and the murders that he had committed but once he was deported back to El Salvador, he paid with his own life since he no longer wanted to continue gang banging.

While I was at Occidental College, MS 13 grew and spiraled out of control. Federal immigration laws had not given these children the opportunity to become permanent residents through refugee status. And now, those kids were no longer kids. They became men and murderers on the streets of Los Angeles. Some had been kidnapped, raped, and forced to fight in the civil war. Some had even been forced to murder their own family members or parents.

They were taught how to decapitate—to chop someone's head off with a machete. Of course, they were the minority but this did indeed occur.

During military operations in small rural villages some of the children were forcefully taken, then sold, or given for adoption in foreign countries.

Once some of them arrived in the United States they were never able to get jobs since they did not have legal residency. Many dropped out of school and contributed to filling up the prisons. Many others died, were put away for life, or were simply deported. Many elected officials and law enforcement agencies thought that the gang problem would disappear, through repressive law enforcement measures. Through repressive measures, the gang problem did not decrease—the number of gangs and gang members actually grew astronomically.

Some other Salvadoran children, of course, chose to study hard and they became outstanding scholars and even valedictorians at their high schools. Some were lucky to obtain permanent residency through expensive legal immigration procedures and many of these children are now grown professional adults in various fields. Some are proud of their Salvadoran heritage while others are ashamed to admit that they have Salvadoran roots. Others have purposely adopted a Mexican/Chicano identity and others have adopted a white identity.

In the 1980s and 1990s the U.S. and Salvadoran governments did not measure the changes that massive deportations from the United States created in Central American countries. The deportation of gang members from the United States to Central America intensified the gang phenomenon in the urban and rural areas of these countries.

The media and some so-called gang experts have exploited and sensationalized this whole process and are calling MS 13, "The World's Most Dangerous Gang." I still believe that it is very difficult to allocate the title of "The World's Most Dangerous Gang" to a specific gang, while ignoring the many other gangs that exist, some of which consist of larger number of members. The Honduran government even went so far as to create a rumor that MS 13 was communicating and making alliances with Middle Eastern terrorists. It is easier to exaggerate and sensationalize this issue instead of funding programs that will help with gang prevention efforts.

Many of these deported Central American gang members had lost their ability to speak Spanish and were at a disadvantage when they arrived in their homelands. There were no programs or jobs available for them. Many created their clicas or new gangs. They expanded the reach of 18th Street, which initially welcomed and recruited centroamericanos by the thousands during the 1980s. MS and 18th Street initially got along, since they both had many Salvadoran members. Eventually, however, they became rivals. Now they have a mini civil war. They should develop a peace truce in order to decrease the violence that continues to impact innocent victims in El Salvador and in the United States.

Ironically, Oxy created a space for me to learn about our politics and history, while hundreds of young centroamericanos were killing each other in the streets of Los Angeles. I joined with others to create a political organization representing the needs of centroamericanos. The result was CASA, the Central American Student Association. It created quite a stir at Oxy among the Latino students who belonged to MEChA/ALAS. They did not understand why we would want to create our own organization, since ALAS meant "Association of Latin American Students."

Bearing in mind that every country in Latin America has its own history, culture and political needs, we convinced MECHA/ALAS that we needed to form this group in order to represent ours. Eventually, student leaders like Angelica Salas (current Executive Director of the Coalition for Humane Immigrant Rights—CHIRLA) became supportive of our efforts and understood our point of view and necessity to have our identity.

While I left to study abroad in Madrid, Spain, two of my Oxy Centroamericano friends took charge of continuing CASA. I was proud to see that other Centroamericano students were taking this organization seriously. In fact, CASA got so much attention that it was featured on the cover of Los Angeles Times Magazine. Our first advisor for CASA was Professor Margaret Crahan and our second advisor was Professor Warren Montag of the Occidental College English Department.

When I returned from studying abroad and learning about Spain's history and politics, I came back with a more balanced world view. I learned so much about European and Spanish history and politics that I was inspired to make a difference once I returned to Occidental College. Things made more sense because I had a better understanding of Spain's perspectives, history, and politics, as well as the role that Spain played in Latin America. I was so inspired that I even thought of starting a Central American Student Association in Spain, but I decided to strengthen CASA at Occidental College, instead.

In my senior year at Occidental College, I decided to become part of the Learning Across Borders (LAB) program created by Meredith Brown (Oxy alum) at CARECEN. After graduating from Oxy, I went to work for free in El

Salvador. I chose to work with the Federation of Cooperatives of El Salvador (FEDECACES).

I travelled the whole country by car, and we visited the most remote villages to explain the concept of remittances, money sent from the United States to El Salvador. We wanted to establish a program where the poor could establish savings accounts to start up their own small businesses. However, I learned a tremendous amount about how the economic system worked in El Salvador. The exploitation of the poor is the common recurring theme.

I met countless campesinos who were so desperate that they believed an "Americano" (me) could help them with money, to obtain a visa, and to find their lost sons or daughters. These are the immigrants who were murdered while crossing Guatemala and Mexico. Those who risked their lives to get to the "Promised Land"—Los Estados Unidos. I saw the pain and anguish of the *ancianos* (senior citizens).

I discovered that the Civil War led to an improvement in some aspects of life in El Salvador but the real economic power was still held by the wealthiest families. The Civil War led to a restructuring of the military and police forces and created more transparency in terms of human rights. The Farabundo Marti Para La Liberacion Nacional (FMLN—a former guerrilla group) became an official political party in 1992.

I learned about the Arena (National Republican Alliance) and the FMLN political parties. I began to understand each side's history. What I did not comprehend was how El Salvador had allowed itself to become an "experiment" for the United States in their fight against so-called Communism.

The poor campesinos were recruited by both sides. It was essentially the poor killing the poor—poor campesino soldiers fighting poor campesino guerillas. The wealthiest Salvadoran families fled to Miami, Florida. Many still live there.

The truth is that more than 80,000 Salvadorans were murdered during this civil war. Sure, each side will justify it. But I do not justify the murder of innocent women, men, and children. Nor can I justify the billions of dollars that the United States spent in financing the military in El Salvador. War becomes a reality when you see five year old children lying dead on the ground—murdered.

This U.S. funding prolonged the war and it created detrimental post-war traumatic conditions for many of those who survived it. Unfortunately, this war primarily impacted children and young adults. Many still carry faces of terror and panic since they witnessed so much brutality. Many families thought that they had escaped violence when they arrived in Los Angeles. They were wrong. They would soon have to witness the L.A. riots and the violence of gangs.

Chapter Six

1992 L.A. Riots—The Fire
Still Burns in Los Angeles

Many people would rather forget that the L.A. riots happened.

Whether you call them civil disobedience, an uprising, a revolt by the people, or simply the riots, too many lives were lost. Simply put, no one really knows when a riot will explode. We should revisit some of the facts that occurred and contributed to create the L.A. Riots.

Following the surprising acquittal on April 29, 1992, of four white LAPD police officers who beat Rodney King, an African American, rioting lasted three days and extended beyond South LA, leaving 58 people dead, 2,400 injured and $1 billion in property damage.

More than 16,000 people were arrested. More than half were Latino and more than a third African American. The Immigration and Customs Enforcement agency (ICE), formerly known as the Immigration and Naturalization Service, deported at least 700 people. Latino leaders decried the LAPD's targeting of immigrants and its apparent violation of a longstanding city ordinance that prevents local police from intervening in immigration cases.

Special Order 40 was implemented in 1979 to prevent collaboration between the police and federal immigration agencies. However, martial law was declared during the L.A. riots, and military authority took control of enforcing and implementing the laws. The dead bodies were placed in public transit buses and transferred to mortuaries.

A usually forgotten fact is that many people were arrested and deported with no due process.

The arrests were rampant, occurring mostly in poor neighborhoods with high concentrations of recent immigrants. The areas mentioned over and over again were South LA and Pico-Union/Westlake. The stereotype has been and continues to be that African Americans are the majority in South L.A. and that Central Americans are also the majority in Pico-Union/Westlake. That was neither the case in 1992 nor today. These diverse areas include residents who are not just African American and Central American. Latinos are now the majority in South Los Angeles and Mexican immigrants have always been the majority in the Pico-Union/Westlake area.

Some elected officials blamed Central Americans for the looting and rioting in Pico-Union/Westlake. This community in 1992 had little political influence and therefore was silent except for one or two Salvadorans who were allowed to emerge as spokespeople through the media. Carlos Vaquerano and Roberto Lovato from the Central American American Resource Center (CA-RECEN) did speak up for the Central American community but their pleas for non- violence were ignored since the looting and attacks continued. Their courage to speak up for their community must be acknowledged. Especially since the Central American community continues to lack a "unified" voice to tackle important issues. This is the responsibility of the new generation—to create new leaders who will advocate for their community. With courage and no fear.

Denouncing the collaboration between INS and the police was not enough by some city leaders. What should have been denounced were the historical and ongoing violations of civil rights in these poor communities, the lack of economic resources and adequate housing, and the outrageous unemployment rates. These, and other factors, are what contributed to the riots.

People in South Los Angeles and other poor communities were fed up with being ignored and constantly harassed by law enforcement authorities. The videotaped beating of Rodney King was clear evidence of police abuse. The feeling of powerlessness and disenfranchisement led to outrage and unfortunately to rioting.

My uncle's store was protected and spared by African American looters in the 1992 riot. They had grown to respect and liked my uncle and family since they treated their customers with respect. My uncle could have chosen to dislike African Americans since he was beaten in the early 1980s by some African American gang members. My uncle and aunt had three children, one of which fell in love and chose to marry an African American young man from the neighborhood. Now we have nephews who are half Salvadoran and half African American. My uncle continues to operate his small store with his family in South Los Angeles. They chose to not move out of South Central Los Angeles.

Chapter Seven

The Environmental Movement

The L.A. riots taught me a lot. I saw how people were beaten during the L.A. riots, especially innocent Latino immigrants who were caught in the middle. They did not speak English and did not even realize that a full riot had erupted. From 1992 on, I knew that I wanted to work on issues of social justice.

While I was volunteering at the Central American Resource Center (CA-RECEN), I learned about a job opening for a New Voter Organizer at the California League of Conservation Voters (CLCV). I applied and I got the job. It was a great opportunity for a young kid who grew up in South LA, where not many opportunities or jobs exist for young people.

I was told that I would be in charge of getting out the Latino vote and helping to train and identify emerging leaders. I hoped that my idealism, enthusiasm, and academic preparation from Occidental College were good enough credentials to show the world that a young man who grew up in adversity could make a difference.

I had learned many lessons from Peter Dreier's classes at Oxy, and I was eager to implement some of the community organizing concepts that I had read about related to Saul Alinsky and the Industrial Areas Foundation (IAF) founded in Chicago.

The IAF community organizing concepts are quite interesting, as are ones from ACORN and the labor movement. They focus on finding common issues that impact community members—developing and implementing community organizing strategies to make social change. Barack Obama used some of these organizing concepts through his community organizer job in Chicago. His base of support were the churches. Obama did in fact use some of the coalition building and fundraising techniques that are learned in community organizing for his historic presidential election. He combined grassroots organizing with high quality technology tools to reach voters.

I was given an opportunity to work with the environmental movement where I was able to implement my community organizing skills. David Allgood, Southern California Director for the California League of Conservation Voters (CLCV) was a great boss and mentor who believed in empowering poor communities. Also, Rampa Hormel, who is a well known environmental activist and philanthropist, was key in helping to support and fund the CLCV New Voter Project.

I was first given the task to identify specific Assembly, State Senate, and Congressional Districts where I could organize and get out the Latino vote.

We chose the San Gabriel Valley districts and the San Pedro/Long Beach districts. We decided to create a steering committee of prominent Latino leaders who would support our efforts. We included top politicos such as Assembly member Antonio Villaraigosa, State Senator Richard Polanco, State Senator Hilda Solis, Assembly member Grace Napolitano, and other prominent individuals who were curious to see what the West Side Environmentalists would do to get the Latino vote.

I did not have a clear strategy at first, but I quickly learned what to do after holding many meetings and poring over several key Get Out the Vote magazines and manuals. I decided that we would do bilingual phone banks, bilingual direct mailings, media outreach, and community forums with the candidates. I went to various cities to create small steering committees to help recruit volunteers.

We decided to target new Latino voters—those who had recently become U.S. Citizens and had just registered to vote. It was a great strategy. We decided to get out the Vote for 5,000 to 10,000 new Latino voters in each cluster of districts. This strategy paid off big time. We helped to mobilize and turn out over 80% of Latino voters, giving the winning edge to key individuals who remain in office in Sacramento and Washington D.C.

My immersion in the environmental movement became a passion and it sharpened my community organizing skills. The hands-on training also helped me develop my expertise in media relations and communications. I also discovered that op-eds (opinion columns in newspapers) do in fact impact public opinion. I became a regular contributing columnist for La Opinion newspaper, the largest Spanish language newspaper in the United States. Monica Lozano, the Publisher of La Opinion has helped to grow the newspaper and has diversified its readership. The majority of readers of La Opinion are from Mexico and Central America and they obtain their local and home country news through La Opinion. Through La Opinion, I was able to publish op-eds (editorials) focused on environmental justice issues.

At CLCV, I began to realize the power of the environmental movement, but I also discovered that many corporations were against any changes in water or air protections because it hurts their profit making machines.

I spent four years with the California League of Conservation Voters and it took me that long to understand the disconnection between large established mainstream environmentalists and the environmental justice groups, many of which operate in survival mode. Many new environmental justice organizations have been created in order to fight for environmental protections for the poor, and minority communities. I believe the disconnection is shrinking. But there is still a class division between the leadership of the mainstream environmental movement and the activist that comes from the environmental justice (EJ) movement. Some progress has been achieved since more mainstream environmental groups have embraced issues from the environmental justice community. The number of environmental justice organizations has grown and the leadership has expanded.

I learned a great deal from David Allgood. A strong supporter of minority rights, he had registered African Americans to vote in the 1960s and had worked with California's great former Speaker of the Assembly, Jesse Unruh.

I still appreciate the opportunity that was given to me when I worked at the California League of Conservation Voters. It was not an easy job, because many Latino elected officials resented the environmentalists and these officials would give me a hard time when I met with them.

I recall a meeting I had with Congresswoman Lucille Roybal-Allard. She started lecturing and scolding me about how the Westside Environmentalist (mainstream environmental groups) had purposely neglected poor minority communities of East L.A. and South LA. I was new to my job when this occurred in 1996 and it was a good lesson in how to listen and learn. Later on, I began to better comprehend. I also began to get angry since I saw the injustices of how poor community members were dying because of environmental contaminations. I would meet people who lived along Wilmington, Harbor Gateway, Long Beach, Southeast Los Angeles, many lived next to freeways or polluting factories. Some were dying of lung cancer.

Some well known, well documented environmental justice struggles include the brave battle waged by the United Farm Workers in the 1970s against pesticides that harmed the health of farm workers. Some of the chemicals used today continue to cause cancer and birth defects. Cesar Chavez and Dolores Huerta were in the forefront of generating social change. Cesar Chavez and Dolores Huerta were the co-founders of the United Farm Workers (UFW). The UFW was a union created to represent and fight for the labor rights of poor farm workers. Cesar was a man of vision, courage, and integrity. He did not fear the power structure since he was sincere in his battles to bring justice for farm workers. He was not in it for the fame, glory or money. He truly dedicated his life for social change.

A fascinating environmental justice organization is Concerned Citizens of South Central. They courageously fought and won to prevent the City of

Los Angeles to locate the LANCER waste incinerator project in South Los Angeles.

Many other examples can be pointed out in different states that show how poor working class people have chosen to unite and mobilize to protect their environment. Changes clearly can be made through advocacy and grassroots mobilization.

The Natural Resources Defense Council (NRDC), Coalition for Clean Air (CCA), Communities for a Better Environment and other well-known environmental groups have conducted studies showing that poor African American and Latino communities are in closest proximity to uncontrolled toxic waste sites. These communities also have the highest death rates due to environmental contamination.

According to a study titled Building Healthy Communities From The Ground Up: "nearly 3 million people in California suffered from symptoms of asthma in 2001, due in part, to the fact that 11 of the nation's 25 worst counties for ozone contamination are in California. In 1996 the estimated risk of a person getting cancer in California due to a lifetime exposure to outdoor air pollutants was 310 times higher than the Federal Clean Air Act goal of 1 person in 1 million. Within (California), Latinos, Asians and African Americans all have higher cancer risks than whites at any income level."

Again, low income communities are the most impacted, and many residents die due to cumulative negative health factors since they live near these industrial facilities and freeways. Through the California League of Conservation Voters we fought many battles and some worthy legislation was approved into law. I am proud of those four magical years. It was my first real job after college.

I was happy, but still sad in some ways. We were fighting to protect our natural environment while our youth was being recruited to join gangs and getting killed in Los Angeles. I struggled with the eternal dilemma among activists: How much time and effort do you spend trying to save the world, while your own family members, friends, and neighbors are dying in the streets, due to "urban environmental violence?"

Do we save endangered species or our inner city youth? Personally, I believe in a balanced approach. Our youth comes first as they are our future, but without clean air or water we will have no future generations. Both topics should be treated seriously, and small gains are better than doing nothing at all. Therefore, I chose to create the Salvadoran American Political Action Committee (SAL-PAC). I wanted to create a voice for Salvadoran Americans.

Randy Jurado Ertll

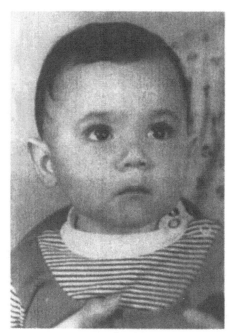

7 months old—
before being deported to El Salvador

My mother when she arrived to the United States

Mama Gume holding my pair of pants
that I wore as a child in Usulutan

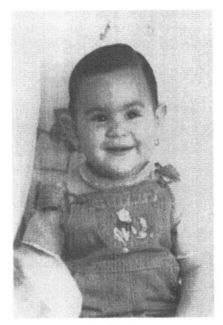

My daughter Mirian

Standing near the National Palace in San Salvador

Mr. O'Brien's third grade class at Menlo Avenue Elementary School

Mr. O'Brien's fourth grade class at Menlo Avenue

Housemates at Rochester Better Chance Program in Minnesota

Working on Capitol Hill (Washington D.C) in Congresswoman Hilda Solis' office

Chapter Eight

SAL-PAC—New Generation of Salvadoran Americans/Overcoming Negative Stereotypes

SAL-PAC (The Salvadoran American Political Action Committee) was an attempt to organize the younger generation of Salvadorenos so they could become more politically involved and help to elect political candidates who took Salvadoran American interests into account.

It was a simple idea that became hope for our community in 1998. It made headlines in the Los Angeles Times and La Opinion newspapers. People were curious to see how 10 to 15 enthusiastic professionals became the Board of Directors of SAL-PAC. I was elected President and it was a great experience. We dedicated our time and efforts on pro bono basis. We chose to focus on raising money and giving it to deserving candidates, whom we endorsed on the basis of a formal interview. The L.A. community began to pay more attention to the needs of Salvadorans now that SAL-PAC was raising money, creating news, and helping elect key candidates.

SAL-PAC only lasted for a couple of years, but we made a strong statement throughout Southern California. Salvadoran Americans/centroamericanos were and are a strong part of the fabric of California. We also were able to demonstrate that we could raise money, mobilize the Latino vote, and help elect non-Salvadorenos like Lou Correa (Orange County), Alex Padilla (former President of the L.A. City Council), former Governor Gray Davis, and former Mayor of Glendale Gus Gomez.

SAL-PAC explored the hope that we could make a difference in the political landscape of Southern California. That hope remains alive and these efforts need to be continued or improved by the new generation of Salvadoran American leaders.

Chapter Nine

Searching for My Roots

After working at CLCV, I went to work as Civic Participation Director for the Central American Resource Center (CARECEN). I wanted to return to doing immigrant rights work and to be closer to the inner city.

The former executive director Angela Sanbrano believed in my abilities and wanted me to work for CARECEN, the largest and most established Central American group in the United States. Angela built CARECEN to a new level and even spearheaded a capital campaign that raised millions of dollars. Now CARECEN owns a three floor building where thousands of children attend to obtain tutoring and computer skills. Angelica Sanbrano, a Mexican American, committed to empowering the Central American community, is a perfect example of how an individual can transcend nationality and become a leader for all communities. CARECEN was established in the early 1980s when waves of Salvadorans, Guatemalans, Hondurans, and Nicaraguans fled to the United States to escape fierce civil wars in their countries. CARECEN was formed in the heart of the Pico-Union/Westlake area. CARECEN was also established in other key cities such as San Francisco, Houston, and Washington D.C.

CARECEN helped thousands of refugees throughout the 1980s and early 1990s. Now CARECEN is led by a young salvadoreno americano, Marvin Andrade, who graduated from USC.

Many horrific stories have been documented by CARECEN staff attorneys. The CARECEN staff attorneys continue fighting for the invisible centroamericanos. In the past, they tried to convince the INS (Immigrations and Naturalization Services) that these individuals were true refugees, and that if they were deported, many would be murdered by the infamous death squads.

Ronald Reagan and his administration did not recognize Central Americans as political refugees. To do so would contradict their foreign policy. The U.S. Government supported the military governments believing that Central-American countries were being influenced by Communist/Socialist movements.

The murder of the highest ranking Catholic official of El Salvador, Archbishop Oscar Arnulfo Romero (R.I.P) was a planned assassination. He was murdered by a hired gun while he was saying mass. The bullet pierced his heart.

My mother had wanted Monsenor Romero to baptize me when I was a baby. Because of scheduling conflicts he was unable to do so. My mother said that he was a quiet and a humble man. She could see his intelligence in his eyes and his authenticity in his smile.

Monsenor Romero continues to be a heroic figure many Salvadorans. He would visit the poor villages and saw firsthand the extreme poverty that children lived in—some were even dying of hunger. He also began to see how the government was killing some of his own friends, other priests. He soon realized that the then President of El Salvador was not his friend, as he once mistakenly assumed.

Monsenor Romero consciously decided to dedicate his life to seeking equality for the poor of El Salvador. He even travelled to the Vatican to seek help from the Pope. His pleas were ignored on purpose. The day before he was murdered, Monsenor Romero publicly demanded that the military stop murdering its own people, especially innocent civilians. He was marked for death through the death squads.

It was a strong message from the military and they truly instilled fear among all Salvadorans. Speak out and you will be killed. The military and National Guard was noted for having kidnapped, raped, and murdered three U.S. nuns and a lay missionary. This situation brought a lot of international attention addressing the lack of personal safety in El Salvador. Human respect was non-existent.

The Salvadoran government knew that the United States would not stop sending military aid. What was going on in El Salvador was inhumane and heartless. After the murder of Archbishop Romero—no one felt safe. Thousands of Salvadorans risked their lives while crossing through Guatemala and Mexico on their way to the United States, to escape the violence. Many were murdered, raped, robbed, and beaten on their way to the United States.

These people fled their own governments in search of safety and respect. However, in their new homes, many experienced challenges. They felt that they could endure anything in order to get to the United States alive. What they did not realize was that the United States did not welcome them.

Many Salvadorans arrived to Los Angeles, half dead. The world famous Salvadoran poet Roque Dalton said that Salvadorans were born half dead. Their hearts had been destroyed after seeing so many gruesome deaths. Their minds had been terrorized by the military and leftist guerillas. If you want to get a graphic picture of what really occurred in El Salvador, read The Massacre at El Mozote book by Mark Danner. That book describes how a whole town was raped and murdered. Even the New York Times verified and documented that such horrific actions were occurring in El Salvador. Of course, the United States was justifying these actions by stating that the military was fighting Communism—with U.S support.

Salvadoran children arrived in the U.S. traumatized and depressed. Some had learned to react to adverse situations through violence. Others had already fought in the civil war (1980-1992) as soldiers and guerillas. Many of these had learned how to handle an M 16 or an AK 47. They knew how to use grenades, Molotov cocktails, and airborne missiles that could shoot down airplanes or helicopters. These children were no joke. They may have been skinny and they may have looked scared, but they were ready to defend themselves, through murder if need be. In the Salvadoran Civil War, these kids were trained and forced to commit horrific murders.

In the United States, many of them were picked on and beaten by the local thugs or gang members. They were made fun of and humiliated in their neighborhoods and schools because of how they spoke and dressed. Children that were 10, 11 or 12 years old were easy recruits for the existing gangs in Los Angeles. Others chose to join the Mara Salvatrucha (MS 13). Many of the initial Salvadoran gang bangers were stoners and they were into heavy metal. They dressed like the heavy metal bands and even took their gang sign to be the sign of the devil, as promoted in heavy metal videos. Some began to carry knives and guns. Once they were picked on, they retaliated with full force and no mercy.

Word started spreading throughout Los Angeles that the Mara Salvatruchas were real crazy. They did get along with 18th Street at first, but by the 1990s the gangs began to feud with each other. The reasons included drug turf issues and personal disputes over the same girl.

These young children were the pioneers of the gang that would grow astronomically. Some older guys that had been in the military or guerrillas also joined and began to run the different clicas. The guys who had belonged to the death squads and army battalions took the MS 13 in an even more violent direction. They called them "los viejitos," the old timers. All gangs knew that messing with MS 13 meant serious problems - death. Many gang members had grown up and seen their own family members raped and murdered in front of them, in El Salvador. Some had been forced to kill their own family members.

During the trainings to become members of the army battalions, such as the Atlacatl Batallion, they were forced to eat live vultures and some drank the blood. Some became so cold that murdering young children became routine. Members of the Atlacatl Batallion were found to be responsible for the murder of six Jesuit priest, their housekeeper and daughter in 1989.

Many kids were forcefully recruited to fight in the war. When these kids arrived in the United States—they were rejected and discriminated in school. They were not treated with dignity and respect. They were seen as the most recent mojados, or "wet backs." The U.S. government did not want to give them permanent residency.

Many went the delinquent and criminal route. They dropped out of school and were drawn by the allure of MS 13. Many Salvadorans also joined other well established and well known gangs, even those dominated by Mexican American or Chicano members. Others joined White Fence, Maravilla, Florencia 13, Harpys/Dead End, Avenues, and other gangs located throughout Los Angeles. Some Salvadorans even joined the predominantly African American gangs: the CRIPS and Bloods. Salvadorans are such a large community that they live throughout Los Angeles County and all over the United States.

It was and still is a demographic myth that Salvadorans are the majority in the Pico-Union Westlake area. Salvadorans mainly settled in the downtown area of Los Angeles and eventually moved to and settled in South Central Los Angeles, South East Los Angeles, the Valley, and other small cities throughout Los Angeles County.

The parents of many of these children are hard workers who found jobs in the garment sweat shops of downtown Los Angeles, worked as janitors or house cleaners, in restaurants as cooks or bus boys, and at other low paying jobs where they are exploited by low wages and no benefits. Yet, because of gang violence, many of these parents have to bury their own sons and daughters. One Salvadoran woman, a student of mine when I taught U.S Citizenship and English as a Second Language to immigrants at Los Angeles High School, confessed to me that she lost her three sons to gang violence. This lady would sometimes come to speak to me at my job at CARECEN. She wanted me to simply listen to her pain and suffering. I empathized with the pain, anguish, and suffering that such mothers carry when their sons or daughters have been murdered.

At CARECEN, I was idealistic and I fought hard to advocate for immigration reform: aNACARA Amendment that would allow not just Nicaraguans, but also Salvadorans, Guatemalans, and Hondurans to obtain their permanent residency. We also urged the school district to complete the Belmont Learning Complex so students could attend.

Construction of the complex was delayed by environmental safety issues; the environmental impact report had not been conducted. We marched, spoke at school board meetings, and fought. Finally, after many years of advocacy and community organizing, LAUSD decided to build another near the Pico-Union/Westlake area.

Today, Belmont High School has a significantly high dropout rate. Many of its students are gang members. It is a school, which like other schools, is supposed to prepare our young adults to succeed at the university level; however, a high number of students fall through the cracks, and become gang members who end up in prison. Belmont High School is not a paradise. It is one of the high schools in the Los Angeles County with many challenges and in need of a lot of change to better serve their young population of students. This is not to disregard that among the thousands of students who graduate from Belmont High School, there are some outstanding alumni.

Chapter Ten

From South L.A. to Capitol Hill

I stayed with CARECEN for only about a year before being recruited to work with Congresswoman Hilda Solis in Washington D.C. as a Communications Director/Legislative Assistant. She is the first Congressional member of Central American descent. Her mother is from Nicaragua and her father from Mexico. She is now the first Latina Congresswoman to become Secretary of Labor, under the President Barack Obama administration. President Obama has created much excitement by selecting Hilda Solis to be Secretary of Labor.

I remember myself, in 2000, being excited about this new opportunity and wondering what it would be like to live and work in Washington D.C. I had saved enough money for my airplane ticket and was eager to begin.

A week before Congress was to reconvene, I moved to D.C. to help set up Congresswoman Hilda Solis' office. I had to get the phone system working and helped to collect resumes that started pouring in. Many people wanted to work with Congresswoman Solis since it was exciting to have another Latina elected from California.

Initially I went looking for apartments with no knowledge of the various neighborhoods and history of each. I was learning how to ride the D.C. metro system. What struck me at first, was that no one speaks to each other in the metro. Unknowingly, I went to some of the worst neighborhoods of Washington D.C.

I also explored other areas and took the metro to see apartments in Suitland, Maryland. This neighborhood is predominantly African American, and I was looking forward to it. However, an opportunity came my way and I moved to an apartment in Adams Morgan. This area is known to be "multicultural" and has a great nightlife and some good food.

The owners of the studio that I found were really cool and they rented me a small space. The rent was extremely high due to gentrification that was occurring in Washington D.C. The demographics of this area had changed dramatically during the 1980s, when Central Americans immigrated to Washington D.C., Virginia, and Maryland.

Today, Salvadorans are the largest immigrant group in Washington D.C. Their political clout is beginning to grow in Virginia and Maryland. They have already elected several prominent Salvadorans. Walter Tejada is Chairman of the Arlington County Board and Ana Sol Gutierrez has been part of the House of Delegates in Maryland and has also served as a school board member. But throughout the 1980s and 1990s, the majority of Salvadorans were ignored and neglected by Capitol Hill and the local and state political machines. Now they are becoming an important community of hard working and entrepreneurial individuals. Salvadorans had to learn to survive on their own. However, the CARECEN D.C., church groups, and the Committee in Solidarity with the People of El Salvador (CISPES) did work hard to help empower Central Americans in the D.C. area.

While I worked for Congresswoman Hilda Solis, I lived near the area where a Salvadoran was shot by a Washington D.C police officer back in 1991. A riot broke out, in the area of Mt. Pleasant, that lasted almost two days due to the antagonistic relationship that existed between the police department and the recent immigrants. Cultural insensitivity and lack of bilingual police officers contributed to this hostile relationship. Many Salvadorans had left violence in their home country and found it again in the United States.

Learning about that riot in 1991 reminded me of the 1992 L.A. riots when Rodney King was savagely beaten by LAPD officers. That incident had brought to light the negative relationship between the immigrant community and the police department of Los Angeles. Similar circumstances existed in the Washington D.C. area.

I cannot help but to revisit the issue of the L.A. riots. They occurred while I was a student at Occidental College.

Then Mayor Tom Bradley and former Chief of Police Daryl Gates did not respond appropriately to the L.A. riots. Many innocent people lost their lives that day, including Latino immigrants who did not know what was going on and were caught in dangerous areas where mobs beat and killed them. The LAPD and National Guard snipers also shot many looters and some civilians.

Those days were horrible. My mother and two sisters had to barricade themselves in my aunt's apartment. Thousands of businesses were burned to the ground, especially the Korean liquor stores.

The L.A. riots exposed the extreme economic gaps that existed in Los Angeles and highlighted how out of touch elected officials were with the realities of the poor neglected African American and Latino communities of South L.A.

Koreans also endured extreme pain and hatred during the L.A. Riots. I was part of a documentary entitled "Wet Sand" produced by DaiSil Kim. She effectively illustrates how Koreans and other communities suffered greatly during the riots. In Washington D.C. I saw similar disparities and challenges that continue to this day in South Central.

One would think that Latino elected officials would work together to improve and empower their own communities but working on Capitol Hill I saw how the Congressional Hispanic Caucus itself was not unified, and how the Hispanic Caucus and Black Congressional Caucus did not communicate enough. I was assigned to be the Hispanic Caucus liaison for Congresswoman Hilda Solis and I was privileged to have been able to participate and attend Congressional Hispanic Caucus meetings. I do have to point out that every community has internal divisions, not just minority communities. But in national politics, divisions are magnified and sometimes are exploited for political purposes.

I was enamored with the grandeur and cultural richness of Washington D.C., but I began to feel lonely. I was used to doing more community work and organizing. I missed Los Angeles. even though I loved the fast pace of Capitol Hill, I decided to return to Los Angeles.

It was such a difficult decision, especially since I had adjusted to first living in Adams Morgan. I also moved to live in Alexandria, Virginia. A kind lady that I met while working on Capitol Hill, Betsy (former press secretary to Congressman Sam Farr), rented me her quiet basement that is located next to a cool railroad where you can see the Amtrak and trains going cross country. You can hear the motors and whistles during the night. It reminded me of the train station exhibits that I would see at the museums located in Exposition Park. I also learned about the history of Alexandria through Betsy's African American neighbors who were from South Carolina and Georgia. Her neighbor, Gene, actually gave me a tour of Alexandria and he showed me the areas where Latinos live.

I was glad that Congresswoman Solis had given me the opportunity to work with her. We pushed for Temporary Protective Status (TPS) for Salvadorans when the earthquakes hit El Salvador. The Congresswoman was seen as a leader on this issue and her involvement became recognized internationally. She is now perceived as a hero in Central American countries. I learned a great deal about how our federal government operates and how legislation becomes law. I also improved my media skills and knowledge at the national level.

It was a difficult decision to leave Washington D.C.

Chapter Eleven

The SANN Year and How I Ended Up Working for the Pasadena Unified School District

I returned to Southern California and went to work for the Salvadoran American National Network (SANN), an umbrella organization that included many prominent Central American/Latino organizations. That same year I also found out that I was going to be a father. I was so proud and happy. My purpose in life began to change. I was no longer just focused on my needs and dreams. I began to understand why I had been writing articles—op-eds (opinion articles) in various newspapers throughout the United States. Why express oneself in a newspaper, giving thousands of people the opportunity to agree or disagree? Writing is like a musician playing his favorite instrument and entertaining a crowd through beautiful melodic songs. Words express much power and can help inspire others to achieve greatness—just like listening to one's favorite song.

After the birth of my daughter, I began to value life more. Now, I work to serve as a protector, mentor, and role model for my child. She is sweet, kind, and intelligent.

I realized that I write to speak through my heart and mind, to express myself in a courageous manner and to inspire younger people to do the same, to leave written material so that my daughter, and others will read it when they are older. I also want future generations of Salvadoran Americans to be proud of their history, heritage, and culture.

Through literature I find happiness and freedom. It creates real satisfaction to see one's written words published in newspapers and magazines, and to see others respond. I especially want to influence young people through what I write.

A song does not have to reach number one status on the Billboard Charts to influence and make people fall in love with each other. I feel the same way with literature; it is an art open to the reader's interpretation. A love letter or romantic poem to one's significant other can influence and create much joy. The written word has an impact, especially when it is written with passion.

We must teach our students in the public school districts that reading and writing are two enabling factors leading to success, which can be accomplished through dedication and practice. At the same time, it is important to take the opportunity to acknowledge those who are bilingual and who overcome the challenges that come with learning a foreign language.

Reading and writing must be taught well at a very young age and it is our responsibility as parents and adults to help inspire our children. Having missed out on *The Cat In The Hat* and other Dr. Seuss books as a child, it was a joy to discover them as an adult. I was especially pleased when I had the opportunity to read a Dr. Seuss book to a first grade class in the Pasadena Unified School District.

I have not forgotten my first book in first grade, *Where The Wild Things Are,* and this book also became my first gift to my daughter. When I opened the book, which I had not seen for decades, it brought back so many wonderful memories. It took me back to my first grade experience at Menlo Ave. School.

My daughter now has a passion for books. That also inspires me to write. I want my daughter to read what I have written and published. I hope that one day she too will be motivated and passionate about writing. She is on the right path. Whether we have children of our own or not, we must ensure that other children learn to read and write correctly at a young age.

This will enhance their ability to attain good jobs in the 21st Century.

Parents must also take proactive measures to help their children become lifelong readers and writers. Just like music, which inspires and gives us hope, reading and writing does the same for millions of children. Just look at the faces of children when they finally learn how to read and write. They smile with joy and feel a great sense of accomplishment. That is why I continue to write. I want my daughter to find joy and hope in reading and writing. I also want young Centro Americanos, Mexico Americanos, and Latinos in general to learn more about each other's history and culture. Learning about each other's culture creates respect to one another, and it also serves as a channel of understanding.

Shortly after I arrived in Los Angeles from Washington D.C., the September 11, 2001 attacks occurred. It was a very tragic experience. That same year one of my friends in Los Angeles, Jaime passed away, leaving behind his dreams for a more inclusive society for undocumented immigrants. I had learned so much from Jaime. He was a humble man who had fought for human rights and social justice for Salvadorans in Los Angeles. *He did not take advantage or make money from his work - he was an unsung hero.* He had a great influence for me and he still motivates me to continue doing good work for the community.

Jaimito taught me that one has to be passionate and truly believe in what you choose to do. I took great pride in the work that I did for the Salvadoran American National Network—we pushed for immigration reform and we were successful in advocating for the renewal of Temporary Protective Status, as well as helping to get the Immigration Department to expedite the NACARA applications. We brought together many community organizations throughout the United States to work together for common goals. Some individuals were not supportive and created other groups, but those groups have since disintegrated. Other disgruntled individuals left SANN and created an organization with a similar name. Their egos and self interests led them to splinter the leadership.

While working with SANN, I took trips to Washington D.C. and to El Salvador to promote policy to improve the lives of Central Americans in the United States. I even organized an official trip to El Salvador with Congresswoman Hilda Solis. Congresswoman Solis was able to meet her family and she began to further discover her roots from Nicaragua.

SANN was not able to sustain funding because a grant from the Ford Foundation was only for one year. I began looking for another job.

I was offered a position as Assistant Director of Communications and Community Relations for the Pasadena Unified School District (PUSD), a school district that was founded in 1874. Ramon (Ray) Cortines was one of the best Superintendents that PUSD has produced. He is now one of the most well-respected and prominent educators throughout the United States. Now we have Superintendent Edwin Diaz who is trying his very best to improve PUSD. We hope that he will be successful in helping to improve the public education for all children in Pasadena, Altadena, and Sierra Madre. At that time, my interest in working for PUSD was strong. In this job, I learned to persevere and not give up despite all the challenges that I faced on a daily basis. I wanted to continue growing as a professional and the Pasadena Unified School District was a good fit at that time. I was competent and committed to make a difference in helping improve the image of the school district. However, after several years, the district's priorities shifted and I was laid off in 2005.

Chapter Twelve

How to Win an Election in the Southeast Los Angeles City of Maywood

After getting laid off from the Pasadena Unified School District, the Los Angeles League of Conservation Voter (LALCV) hired me as a consultant. Through hard work and my-experience of getting out the vote, an unprecedented campaign occurred in the City of Maywood. The Los Angeles League of Conservation Voters endorsed city council candidates and it was an overwhelming environmental victory.

The City of Maywood is one of the smallest and most over populated cities in California. Though small in geographic size, it can no longer be ignored because it has obtained so much media attention. We made history when the environmentalists took on entrenched political interests that were opposed to environmental protection.

The community of Maywood now serves as a model of how environmental issues can indeed motivate people to vote in high numbers to protect the air and clean the drinking water. We proved that disadvantage people can be mobilized and empower themselves.

Environmental issues, promoted by the L.A. League of Conservation Voters, were what won the Maywood elections. Police brutality, inadequate housing, and various propositions on the November 2005 ballots also motivated people to vote. Environmental protection is a top issue of concern for California Latinos.

Latinos in California have always taken an interest in environmental protection. The California League of Conservation Voters (CLCV) sponsored a poll in 1996 and found that the Latino electorate truly cared about clean air and clean water issues, as well as the creation of safe parks.

In 1996, through CLCV we won several State Assembly, State Senate, and Congressional seats. Through the New Voter Organizing Project, we crafted bilingual phone banks and direct mailings together with candidate community

51

forums that emphasized environmental protection. CLCV helped to mobilize new Latino voters and the turnout was in the range of 70% to 80%.

The model used in the 1996 election cycle proved to also be effective at the local level in the City of Maywood. Updated voter lists were used for the November 8, 2005 Maywood elections, and a committed cadre of 40 to 50 volunteers from Padres Unidos de Maywood (PUMAs) helped to operate bilingual phone banks and ensure consistent precinct walking.

Precinct leaders were identified and trained to get out the vote. Media coverage of this race helped inform Maywood residents about the candidate's positions on environmental protection.

There were two especially popular actions that helped get out the vote. The legendary Dolores Huerta (co-founder of the United Farm Workers) came to support us and thousands of people came out onto the streets to see the caravan that Dolores was leading. She is a humble and authentic leader and I admire her greatly. After the visit from Dolores Huerta, the enthusiasm and commitment from the volunteers was palpable. The residents of Maywood clearly wanted a change in leadership at city hall. They were demanding clean water and the creation of more park space.

The federal government identified a Superfund site known as PEMACO in this small, densely populated city, a site that is considered one of the five most contaminated in the country. The new city council members must now find ways to fully cleanup the PEMACO site and obtain community input. Community members must take part in the discussions, plans, and options for the site. The Maywood electorate had hoped that these newly elected officials will help protect the environment in Maywood and advocate for respect from the police. With the new city council leadership, Maywood community members must be invited to get more involved with issues such as PEMACO and creation of park space.

Now, the City of Maywood has a tremendous opportunity to find creative ways of addressing environmental cleanup and protection issues. The city can become the environmental protection champion of Southeast Los Angeles and set an example. The City of Maywood is a case study establishing that environmental issues do resonate with voters and that people will get out to vote in order to protect the air they breathe and the water they drink. This historical victory can now be replicated in other small and medium size cities throughout Los Angeles County and beyond. Low-income individuals can be motivated to vote through grassroots and electoral campaign organizing stimulated with a message of environmental protection.

Chapter Thirteen

El Centro de Accion Social

Several things drew me to Pasadena. From the time I was in elementary school I took a strong liking to Albert Einstein, who at one time taught at Cal Tech in Pasadena. I also read the free magazine called "The Plain Truth," whose founder eventually moved to Pasadena. As a student at Occidental College, I would sometimes visit Pasadena. But I never imagined that my career trajectory would take me there.

The phone call that I received in 2005 from El Centro de Accion Social's Board President, Gloria Delaney, is still vivid in my mind. She called to ask me if I was interested in applying for the Executive Director position. I thought about it for a minute and I said yes. Ray Cortines, current Superintendent of Schools for the Los Angeles Unified School District and Dolores Huerta, co-founder of the United Farm Workers (UFW) were also supportive of me obtaining the job at El Centro. Dolores Huerta even took the time to directly call Gloria Delaney, President of the Board, to directly endorse and to make a strong recommendation for me. I will forever be grateful to Ms. Huerta.

Sometimes, it seems that one's destiny is already determined. Kids who are trying to make it out of war zones learn to create their own destiny because there is no one available to extend a helping hand. I was fortunate to have wonderful individuals who extended a helping hand to me. Sometimes a strong belief and faith in religion helps us to get through trying times. God is what helps many individuals to overcome insurmountable challenges. A strong will to live and not losing hope is critical to keep going.

Despite its over 40-year track record, El Centro de Accion Social has largely gone unnoticed in Los Angeles, in part, because it is located in Pasadena.

El Centro is the oldest Latino organizations in the Pasadena area and it was founded to help the poor Latino community in the San Gabriel Valley, with a special emphasis on programs to enhance the education and the lives of youth. The organization has touched the lives of thousands of individuals, and still plays a key role in public affairs in Pasadena and the San Gabriel Valley area.

I believe that Chicanos, Mexicanos, Salvadorenos, and all Latinos have some differences, but the similar struggles, and common issues, can help to unite these diverse communities. We can even see ourselves as related if we consider the historical mobility of the Aztecs, Mayas, and Incas. It is great when one is accepted and respected as an individual who can transcend a nationality or ethnic group. We must strive to accept and understand our differences too, because they enrich our diverse cultures. We just need to be willing to explore and get to know other communities. We must not be satisfied with simply accepting and admiring our own roots.

By serving as Executive Director of El Centro, I feel I can serve as a positive role model for youth and lend a hand to our senior citizens. I can raise funds for worthy projects that help the low-income Latino community. I work hard to raise money from various foundations, corporations, and individual donors. Leading a non-profit community organization is not for the faint of heart. The work is very demanding but in the end countless children and families benefit. When I started working at El Centro, Frank Quevedo and Fernando DeNecochea from Southern California Edison, were the first corporate leaders to agree to be a corporate sponsor and big supporter. I still appreciate their friendship and wise counsel. It is tremendously fulfilling when we see our students succeed and graduate from high school. We have developed a scholarship fund for those who enroll at Pasadena City College (PCC) and other institutions of higher learning.

El Centro will continue to play a key role and continue to change lives for the better. Just like the scholarship program A Better Chance, El Centro was based on a simple idea: to help students to obtain a quality education. I was fortunate that A Better Chance saved me. I am trying to help others who face similar challenges and I feel that it is my turn to give back to the community.

I know that many individuals who work in city government, school districts, and police departments truly care and do great work to help neglected and ignored communities. I don't want youth to be abused and victimized by careless adults who work in these entities, which are supported by tax-payer dollars.

The challenges faced by children and families who live in extreme poverty in Latin America are quite different when they come to the United States. Many opportunities do exist in the United States, but it seems that young people often choose a path of darkness since they are not aware of the consequences of joining a gang or dropping out of school. How to tackle the issues of violence and gangs is constantly debated. Community organizations and government must do more to address these tough issues. We can no longer ignore young men and women who are at risk to joining gangs.

We have to help through both prevention and intervention programs. Suppressive measures from law enforcement are not enough. Community groups, city officials, school districts, law enforcement, and our federal government must work together to make our communities safer, and we must create more programs and opportunities for our youth. We are not asking for government handouts but real support. El Centro is thankful to various Foundations that have been extremely supportive: The California Endowment, The Wellness Foundation, Kaiser Foundation, Ahmanson Foundation, Parsons Foundation, Rose Hills Foundation, Pasadena Community Foundation, McCormick Tribune Foundation, Dwight Stuart Youth Foundation, Weingart Foundation, United Latino Fund, Tournament of Roses Foundation, Union Bank Foundation, and Mustangs on the Move among many others that have been generous.

The founders of El Centro de Action Social helped create a model of a community organization that has withstood the test of time. El Centro has improved many lives, and many of its staff members, former executive directors, and board members have given a lot to make a difference in the lives of children, as well as senior citizens.

El Centro de Accion Social plays a key role in helping many youth and senior citizens. We need more such community based organizations to advocate for the rights of poor community members. Serafin Espinoza, former Director of Villa Parke Community Center was instrumental in partnering and supporting the efforts of El Centro. He is one of the pioneers in fighting for Latino rights in Pasadena, along with countless other individuals. Pasadena Mayor Bill Bogaard and Bernard Melekian, who is Chief of Police clearly understands the powerful relationship that city government and community based organizations must have to improve society. Mayor Bogaard has been and still is a strong supporter and champion of El Centro de Accion Social.

I also need to mention the great leadership of Congressman Adam Schiff who has always been supportive and a strong advocate/champion in support of El Centro's youth. He secured appropriations/earmarks funds for El Centro de Accion Social to further grow and strengthen its youth education programs. These Federal funds are fundamental for El Centro to help more young students through quality and effective programs.

I appreciate and I am deeply grateful to Gloria Delaney and the board of directors who gave me the opportunity at being Executive Director of El Centro de Accion Social—making me the first executive director of Salvadoran descent. Gloria Delaney recently passed away in January 2009, but we will keep her in our hearts and mind. She mentored and helped me tremendously. She was a just, firm, and tough lady that we will miss dearly. Board President Norma Kachigian has also dedicated much time, kindness, and passion in empowering El Centro.

They have trusted my experience and commitment to help those in need.

Chapter Fourteen

American Me, the Sopranos, and the National Geographic Channel

Chicanos and Salvatruchas have a lot in common and I am not referring to a gangster lifestyle. We Latinos also have a lot in common with African Americans, because of our shared history of political struggles. We faced colonization, destruction of our indigenous roots, and the shame that has been placed upon us by the mainstream media that continue to portray us as servants and criminals. Both African Americans in the United States and our indigenous ancestors in Latin America were slaves. Many indigenous people were exploited and forced to work the lands that were forcefully taken away from them. Many indigenous tribes were used by the Spanish colonizers to fight each other—this has been well documented by studying the Aztec and Inca empires.

Latinos and African Americans who obtain an education and begin to experience power and prestige should make a commitment to help their own communities. In addition, each individual must examine and discard the self hatred mentality. Latinos and African Americans who take advantage and oppress their own communities should be ashamed and exposed.

Along similar lines, when an ethnic group has a few Hollywood stars, it often does not trickle down to the masses. We need more positive role models in mainstream TV shows that will not perpetuate an image of criminality or ignorance. Enough of negative stereotypes. We don't want our young kids trying to imitate scenes from movies like "American Me" and trying to become like television characters such as Tony Soprano. Also, our Latina youth need more positive Latina role models on TV. Sometimes they are also negatively influenced by the promotion of the gangster lifestyle promoted on television programs, Hollywood films, and English or Spanish music videos.

The negative cycle becomes self fulfilling, and the youth begin to fantasize about becoming part of the gangster or illicit lifestyle.

Crimes committed by a few young Salvadoran gang members continue to tarnish the image of hard-working, tax-paying, law-abiding Salvadorans who live such states as California, Texas, Virginia, Maryland, Washington D.C., and many other states. In fact, Salvadorans are the largest Latino immigrant group living in Virginia, Washington D.C, Maryland, San Francisco, and the Boston area. They have a high rate of employment, are known to be savvy business owners. Many Salvadorans have not been informed about government programs and they have not applied to obtain help. Most have worked hard, have saved money, bought a home and many started their own small businesses. They have a tradition of being entrepreneurs.

In part, because of the criminal activities of the gang MS-13, Salvadoran Americans have become stereotypically associated with gangs. Of course, obsessive media coverage has also contributed to reiterate a negative image of Salvadorans/Latinos. These obsessive media coverage has further promoted gangs and some youth actually begin to fantasize about being part of the gangster lifestyle.

We must teach the new generation of Salvadoran Americans that nonviolence should be sought after, pursued, and adopted. Young Salvadorans must learn about the teachings from Mahatma Gandhi, Martin Luther King Jr., Cesar Chavez, and from Archbishop Oscar Romero, some of which lost their lives while advocating nonviolence and respect for all people. The government of El Salvador must invest in gang prevention, social programs, and in education in order to create professionals among the poor youth. Otherwise, the cycle of violence will continue given limited opportunities and jobs in El Salvador.

A successful Salvadoran American civil rights attorney in the United States can tremendously help his own ethnic community achieve success in American society. One should not seek respect and self-importance by killing one's own people or innocent victims. One can gain respect through academics and learning about one's own history and roots. This can create a source of positive self-worth and counteract self hatred.

Be it Mexican or Salvadoran, the formation of gangs seems to share one component: a search for respect in a society. In addition, a big challenge for Salvadoran youth was co-existing with Chicano and African American gangs. The response to this challenge was unfortunately one that embraced violence.

Violence was also sometimes perpetuated at the family level, partly because the cruelties of the civil war instilled fear, oppression, and anger in the hearts of the population.

For the last couple of decades, the U.S. government has been deporting gang members, to their home countries, including El Salvador. This contributed in an amazing growth of gangs in Mexico and Central America. Clearly, the problem has not been resolved, just exported.

Elected officials don't seem to have solid plans to help the thousands of young Salvadorans who live throughout the United States. Establishing positions of gang czars is not enough. Suppression and enforcement are not enough. Programs that focus on intervention are key to deterring the youth from joining gangs. The Attorney General's office from the state of Virginia is beginning to obtain Federal funding through the Office of Juvenile Justice and Delinquency Prevention—to focus on gang prevention efforts.

However, a further step in the right direction would be job-skills training and job creation for Salvadoran youths. A prosperous future should be ensured through education and jobs, not by joining a gang or becoming a prison statistic.

Government, churches, businesses, community nonprofits, and other entities must--*must*--help to train and create jobs for our young generation. We must do this now or the problems will continue to proliferate. Let's roll up our sleeves and begin to help our youth. We cannot afford to lose another generation to violence and drugs.

We also have to hold the media accountable for how they portray Salvadorans/ Central Americans and Latinos in general.

For example, the Salvadoran American Political Action Committee (SALPAC) courageously brought to the attention to NBC studios, that they touted "Will & Grace" as a show that embraced diversity, while a Salvadoran maid on the show was referred to by another character as "tamale." We were successful in denouncing this negative portrayal of a Salvadoran female representation.

The TV program, "The Sopranos" had a major influence on the mindset of Americans. It portrayed the Italian Mafia in an interesting manner with scripts that were original, with no politically correct rhetoric. Most of us liked it and we fell under the allure of gangsters. Some members of the Italian American community did protest the portrayal of their community in The Sopranos. Many Salvadoran and non Salvadoran youth are now trying to imitate that program. The Godfather also played a prominent role in the mindset of its viewers. Now many Salvadoran gang members are collecting "taxes" from small business owners, street vendors, or bus drivers in El Salvador.

Chicanos, Salvadorans (Central Americans), Puerto Ricans, Cubans, and Dominicans face an uphill battle in the way they are depicted. Sometimes they even fall into the trap of imitating the negative stereotype, common in the way their communities are portrayed on TV or music videos. Producers, directors, and actors become rich in promoting these stereotypes, which represent violence and negative roles, thereby misrepresenting whole communities.

I'm not saying that all youth become gang members because of these programs. But it is a fact that youth are impressionable and many times they want to imitate what they see on television or movies.

Many Chicanos are characterized as small-time gangsters, while Salvadorans are often portrayed as drug kingpins in TV shows like "The Shield." In addition, in the movie Training Day, actor Denzel Washington refers to the Salvadoran gang—Mara Salvatrucha, when he points out some gang members in a movie scene where they are drug dealing. This further reinforces how Hollywood is now incorporating MS 13 into their movie scripts.

Unfortunately, glamorizing, or simply focusing on these images are what many youngsters want to emulate. We must demand that the major TV channels, producers, and directors create characters that will give pride and honor to a Mexican American, Chicano, Salvadoreno, Centro Americano, Sur Americano, Cubano or Puerto Riqueno. Enough of the stereotypes on television programs that portray Latinos and African Americans as drug dealers, gang members, and prone to violence.

We have to teach our children that they must strive to become professionals by attending institutions of higher learning or trade and technical schools.

The Salvadoran Mauricio Cienfuegos, a former major league soccer player with the Los Angeles Galaxy, remains a superstar among Latinos. A humble and charismatic individual, who has not forgotten his roots, he gives back to the community and serves as a positive role model.

We also should recognize the contributions made by former State Senator Liz Figueroa, who was the highest ranking Salvadoran American elected official in California. She was an effective legislator fighting for environmental protection, health care access, and other important social issues.

A recognized Salvadoran, Chicano group of performers are the members of Culture Clash, which is a nationally known theater performance group that includes one Chicano and two Salvadorans. A source of Latino pride, they are committed to helping their communities, through humor and entertainment. They agreed to do a benefit performance for El Centro de Accion Social at the Pasadena Playhouse in 2007. They were wonderful and we sold out the show. The funds raised were used to hire additional staff at El Centro.

We have to secure a critical mass of such profesionales who will help their own community members and who will also serve as positive role models. Who are willing to give back to their community through volunteering or serving as mentors.

When I had just arrived as a child from El Salvador, I would watch the National Geographic Channel. Coming from a magical place surrounded by nature, trees, and humming birds, I loved nature. More than three decades later, I find myself in another magical place, Los Angeles/Pasadena but now I see, with disappointment, how The National Geographic Channel has also chosen to stereotype Salvadorans.

Salvadorenos were notoriously featured on the National Geographic Channel, in a so-called investigative program entitled "The World's Most Dangerous Gang." They focused on the infamous Mara Salvatrucha (MS 13) and they gave it that title. Now a whole new generation of Salvadorans wants to identify itself with La Mara or EMESE. These types of documentaries create a "self-fulfilling prophecy." Since youth hear that MS 13 is so violent—they feel that they have to imitate and surpass other acts of violence.

I only hope and dream that one day, we will be featured on the National Geographic Channel or Public Broadcasting Service (PBS's) American Experience as a productive, entrepreneurial, resourceful, courageous, and positive community of Salvadorenos, whose hard labor has contributed to making America a better place. We have to further promote the positive historical contributions that Salvadorans have made and have gone unnoticed.

I should also note an amazing act of courage that has not received the attention it deserves from the History Channel or other prominent television programs: The government of El Salvador saved the lives of over 40,000 Hungarian Jews in 1944.

Dec. 16 marks the anniversary of the Battle of the Bulge, where the Allied forces turned the tide against Hitler's evil forces in 1944.

Unfortunately, millions of Jews had already been murdered throughout Europe by then.

As we remember the valiant battle against Hitler, we also should note an amazing act of courage that has not received the attention it deserves: The government of El Salvador saved the lives of more than 40,000 Hungarian Jews that same year.

Working through its consular office in Geneva, the Salvadoran government came up with a creative plan. It decided to issue Salvadoran citizenship papers to Hungarian Jews who would otherwise have been sent to Nazi death camps.

The authors of this plan were Salvadoran Consul Col. Jose Arturo Castellanos and First Secretary/Honorary Consul George Mantello, who was of Jewish ancestry.

Mantello, whose original name was Mandl, spoke no Spanish and never set foot in El Salvador. But he was friends with Castellanos, and Castellanos contributed with the humane act to save lives. He gave Mantello his honorary position at the embassy. Mantello used it to publicize Nazi atrocities and then came up with the idea of offering citizenship to Hungarian Jews. Castellanos embraced Mantello's efforts and Castellanos convinced the Salvadoran government to go along.

In Budapest, tens of thousands of Hungarians Jews were able to obtain Salvadoran citizenship papers free of charge. These were crucial for escaping the Nazi concentration camps and certain death.

Thanks to Castellanos and Mantello, El Salvador was the only country that offered nationality rights to Hungarian Jews on a massive scale during World War II.

Castellanos and Mantello deserve to be remembered as heroes. Let us follow their example by assisting those within our own country who face deportation or oppression. Of course, immigrants in the United States facing deportation are not nearly in the same kind of situation that Jews were in during World War II. But the example of reaching across nationalities and across religions to assist fellow human beings in need is one that we all can take to heart.

It is important to remember the humanistic actions certain governments around the world have taken to protect the human race. Colonel Jose Arturo Castellanos and Consul George Mantello serve as amazing role models who chose to take action during a time of tragedy.

Colonel Jose Arturo Castellanos and George Mantello deserve to be recognized and remembered as heroes. They truly set the example that few individuals can make a difference.

Salvadorans and Jews need to develop coalitions in Los Angeles and in other parts of the United States. We must teach our students about the role that El Salvador played during World War II.

We need to help our young men and women, who are of Salvadoran descent, learn more about their own history and how El Salvador has played a key role in having saved so many lives. Even though El Salvador's past is filled with a violence, the overall history of El Salvador goes beyond violence.

The Central American Studies (CAS) program established at Cal State Northridge must be replicated and created at other College/University campuses. Our students must learn about their own history and culture. Professor Beatriz Cortez, Professor Carranza, along with other key professors are making a fundamental difference by helping to teach our future generation of Central American leaders.

We also have to teach ourselves about the Aztec, Mayan (Pipil) history. How much do we have in common? Why different nationalities need to get along and need to continue building bridges, communication, respect, and trust with our African American, Middle Eastern, Asian, and Anglo brothers and sisters. After all, we are all related somehow in the distant past through our genes.

Latinos and African Americans obtaining Bachelor of Arts, Masters, or Ph.D. degrees should return to their communities and give back. They must share their knowledge and experiences. They should come back to mentor and tutor young students. An inner city "Peace Corps" is definitely needed, throughout the United States. We must get motivated college/university students to work in disenfranchised communities, for example through community organizing campaigns. These organizing campaigns can focus on job creation and training programs, similar to the Los Angeles Conservation Corps. These efforts will help to reduce gang involvement and violence in our inner cities.

Let's stop the violence and adopt a philosophy of non-violence.

We should not allow immigrant children to be mistreated, deported, beaten, and abused. Let's protect everyone's civil rights as human rights. To borrow from the late Marvin Gaye, "don't punish me with brutality." In the memory of all the murdered youth and innocent civilians, let's stop and ask "What's Going On?" We should take action, get involved, and make a difference. Let's not be complacent and accept a violent world.

We need to change minds and souls. We need our men and women to become "Peace Ambassadors" at home, in their communities, schools, and at work. However, it is up to each individual if they want to follow this path. Being responsible is essential towards accomplishing goals and becoming a person of self-worth.

Chapter Fifteen

Perseverance

Writing a book about one's personal challenges is not easy. But I felt compelled to share some of my experiences in life so our youth could more easily believe in themselves and not give up on their dreams; even when insurmountable obstacles are placed in their path. We cannot victimize ourselves. My story is not the only one of struggle—many other children have faced worse experiences in their lives.

However, I learned at a young age that perseverance is fundamental leading to success. But more importantly, spirituality has been a powerful tool in my life. You can be spiritual and real at the same time. Seeing the injustices that occurred in El Salvador and the United States has driven me to help other people improve their lives. I have seen people lose their lives and now I want to help save lives through action, and in part, through the written word. I hope that one of my experiences or stories will capture the attention and hopefully positively influence young people so that they can improve their lives. But we have to be realistic about how we approach our own lives.

I am sharing the story of how immigrant children struggled and survived during the turbulent civil war of El Salvador and other Central-American countries. Other young children experienced violence, poverty, and oppression. The challenges they faced in the United States were often based on their nationality, skin color, and inability to speak English, which contributed to the humiliation that they endured. Many youth continue to suffer by having cruel and inhumane role models within their own homes, schools, and community. Some adults are predators and they prey on innocent children. Many children are used as drug dealers and they are taught by their parents how to steal and commit other types of crimes.

I was a "minority within a minority" since I chose the path of "light" and not "darkness." I chose to study and obtain an education. However, I did not make it alone—many kind souls helped me. Nevertheless, every day continues to be a struggle for me, to stay motivated and to uplift others.

The programs I was involved in, such as the LAPD Explorers, A Better Chance, and Outward Bound, and the mixed martial arts activities helped shape who I am today. Through Brazilian Jui-Jitsu (Machado Academy) you can get physically in shape, sharpen your mind through the grappling/lock techniques, and you gain more overall confidence. I hope that other students will consider searching the internet for these programs and consider them. It may improve or change lives for the better. I was fortunate to find and participate in these programs.

I still feel sorrow for my friends who did not make it alive out of El Salvador and South Central. I know that it is not my fault, but I share the pain of memories. I have to live with those memories but I have chosen to leave the negative experiences in the past and move forward.

Programs such as those I have participated in are critical for students to change their lives and succeed. Regrettably, these programs can only help a small percentage of disadvantaged, minority students, but it's better than having no programs at all. In fact, we need to do a better job of informing students that certain programs do in fact exist to help them.

We need foundations, corporations, school districts, city government, community-based organizations, churches, law enforcement, and other entities to make investing in our youth a priority. We need gang prevention and intervention programs that are efficient and that can truly help young kids stay away from gangs. Father Greg Boyle from Homeboy Industries in the Los Angeles area, for example, has developed a great model of job creation that can be replicated in other cities. He raised funds to create businesses that produce tortillas, bakery, and he helped to establish cafes/restaurants where former gang members can obtain a job. Father Boyle also sends, willing gang members, to obtain work related skills at L.A. Trade Technical School. There, they learn how to become chefs. His model can be replicated in other cities throughout the United States.

Too many students are suffering from post traumatic stress disorder and depression due to the challenges faced in poor neighborhoods: inefficient schools, and high crime rates. Lack of opportunities helps create hopelessness. The bottom line is that we need to offer a quality education to all children in the United States. Hard-working, low-income people demand our attention, whether they live in Northwest Pasadena or South Central Los Angeles. They cannot remain invisible.

We need drastic improvement or changes in leadership to improve South Central Los Angeles, which is plagued by many of the same problems that existed in the 1980s. Demographics have changed it from being predominantly African American to now being predominantly Latino. However, gang activity, homicides, drug sales, astronomical school drop-out rates, teen pregnancies and high unemployment remain rampant. Some elected officials chose to change the name from "South Central" to "South L.A." but the underlying problems, which are chronic poverty and low education levels, has not changed much in this geographic area.

It has been documented that some of the worst schools in South Los Angeles are located a few blocks away from the prestigious University of Southern California (USC). I still remember how the security guards would ask what we were doing hanging around the campus and sometimes if we had our bikes they would ask us to leave. Not politely but with bad words.

Fortunately, USC is now more involved in South Los Angeles, but they can do more. The Education Department there can help the struggling middle and high schools that are near USC by assisting them in implement effective educational curriculums and resources. USC students and faculty can become more involved by serving as tutors or mentors for low income, minority students that live and attend schools around USC. Some of these activities or community services are already being implemented in certain schools such as the Foshay Learning Center.

However, most of these schools near USC, in South L.A., do not get adequate State funding, and as a result, most of the students there can only dream of attending USC. The drop-out rates of students who attend public schools in South Central are unacceptable.

A study conducted by Harvard University found that nearly half of the students at South Central's Manual Arts High School and Jefferson High School drop out of school. I attended both of these schools, so I know the sad realities. Of course, research institutions, think tanks, and statisticians can refute and question drop-out rates. Sometimes drop outs are categorized as truant. The sad reality is that dropout rates within these high schools continue to be in the double digits.

We must continue to advocate for the students of South LA, and they must learn to become leaders and to speak up for their social and human rights. It requires a fair distribution of resources to inner-city schools and a greater commitment to quality education for all. The youth of South Central deserve more qualified and caring teachers and more dedicated principals. We cannot set low expectations for our students or accept mediocre performance. Parent involvement is also critical.

The education issue is one that should unite African Americans and Latinos. We should not be fighting for the same crumbs. Both communities have to work together to demand equity in the distribution of resources.

We must not condemn, be judgmental, or quick to crucify—especially if we have not walked in the shoes of the hopeless and despairing.

One day it may be our own self who falls.

I grew up in turbulence and witnessed violence—just like thousands of other children—but I have not lost hope. Let's stop being cynical and skeptical—become an active citizen in civil society to make a difference. I was fortunate to have taken part in several programs that taught me a lot about life.

My mother always told me to "be original" and to not imitate others. She is a wise woman. I never wanted to let my mom down, therefore, I struggled and fought to obtain an education. And man, it was not an easy road to take. It's easier to be tempted to get involved in negative activities, especially through wicked friends.

If that young man or woman falls—let's help them to get up again—to stand up with dignity y respeto propio.

Chapter Sixteen

Lessons Learned, the Future, and Conclusion: Wake Up Everybody

It has not been easy to remember some of the episodes of my life that I felt compelled to share. Some of the same issues that I confronted while growing up continue to impact thousands of other youth in South Central Los Angeles. Many are still faced with living in neighborhoods that are full of drugs, violence, and gangs.

Some of the lessons that life has taught me are that we have to learn from our mistakes and not repeat them. However, sometimes we may repeat them—but each time we must learn a lesson. We have to learn to forgive our own selves and to not live in shame.

We cannot completely forget or ignore the past and we should not forget the lessons that we learn through pain and suffering. However, we have to share those experiences in a responsible manner and not allow ourselves to be used by others. Some self help programs are practically businesses who want to make profit from individual's pain and suffering.

There are so many leadership seminars out there that supposedly help teach us how to become leaders or better people. Many of these seminars charge hefty amounts of money and they really don't care about the long term personal well being of the individual. What they truly want is to make profit from the pain and suffering of many needy individuals who are willing to spill their guts in front of others to obtain comfort. We see how individuals humiliate themselves by going on national television shows and exposing their deepest secrets. Then they return to their own communities and nothing is resolved but they have exposed their vulnerabilities. When they return to their communities—others gossip or make fun of them instead of uplifting them or providing a helping hand. Sometimes when you are "down and out"—there is no help.

They see no interest or self gain from someone who is monetarily broke or emotionally in pain.

We hope that President Barack Obama will invest in and hold accountable city governments, state governments, and community based organizations that receive federal funding. Various cities and community based organizations must prove that they in fact are making a difference in helping youth. Tax payers must also be vigilant about how funds are being distributed for various projects and must demand that tax payer funds be invested in youth education and other programs that will improve our neighborhoods — whether we live in poor, middle class, or rich communities.

President Barack Obama has taught us a meaningful lesson — that we can in fact make our dreams a reality if we work hard enough, respect others, and do what is correct as an individual. Of course, we will make mistakes along the way, but we must put aside our personal selfish interests and work towards improving our own families and communities. Monetary gain creates only partial happiness.

Sometimes our own family members will make mistakes and we ourselves will also make mistakes or errors in judgment. Sometimes our sons and daughters will be tempted to join a gang or to engage in illegal activities, such as experimenting with drugs. We have to teach our children that getting involved in these illegal activities is no joke and that the consequences can lead to death or self destruction.

Growing up in South Central Los Angeles and El Salvador was no piece of cake. Today, I am blessed to have lived this long and I know that I can still make a difference in helping others. I don't know for certain where I will be in the future or what I will have accomplished. All I know is that I am trying to make a difference in the lives of hundreds of students and other individuals through my work at El Centro de Accion Social.

I recently traveled to El Salvador and I visited my grandmother. I hugged her frail body. I began to remember all of the injustices. I still see the pain in my people; I see their scars, their troubled faces, their looks of anguish. I also see the beautiful children. They remind me that there is still hope and that a new generation of Salvadorans can make El Salvador a better country. A generation of new Salvadoran American leaders in the United States must also help to uplift and improve their own communities. They have to take personal responsibility in helping themselves and others. We must not allow more children to be murdered or our youth to be incarcerated for life.

I have also chosen to write this book for the young generation of Latinos and non Latinos who will face tough choices in their lives. Some will be faced with living in a domestic violence household, others with sexual abuse, some will be pressured to join a gang, some will be tempted to experiment with drugs, and others will continue to face many serious obstacles.

Courageous individuals will choose to ignore their violent environment and will make a conscious choice to focus on reading, writing, and doing well in school, to become eligible to attend a college or university or to obtain a job through a technical training program.

We have to learn to not be judgmental and adopt the philosophy of non-violence.

Unfortunately the violence continues. But let's teach our children to respect and help others who are in need, especially those who are suffering.

This book is for those young men and women who are blessed and do not have to face awful experiences and for those of us who have had to face insurmountable struggles and pain in our lives. Even though we carry struggle, today is a good opportunity to get rid of that pain and walk free—with heads held high. I tell kids to never ever let anyone step on them or put them down. Instead, get rid of fear, stand up to injustices.

Made in the USA
San Bernardino, CA
13 November 2014